"Jesus Said..."

Unless otherwise indicated, Scripture quotations are taken from the *New King James Version*. Copyright © 1979, 1980, 1982, 1990, 1995, Thomas Nelson, Inc., Publishers.

Scripture quotations marked *KJV* are taken from the King James Version of the Bible.

Scripture quotations marked *NIV* are taken from *The Holy Bible, New International Version®*. NIV®. Copyright © 1973, 1978, 1984, 2011 by International Bible Society. Used by permission of Zondervan Publishing House. All rights reserved.

Scripture quotations marked *NASB* are taken from the *New American Standard Bible®*. Copyright © The Lockman Foundation 1960, 1962, 1963, 1968, 1971, 1972, 1973, 1975, 1977, 1995. Used by permission.

Scripture quotations marked NLT are taken from the *Holy Bible, New Living Translation*, copyright © 1996, 2004, 2007, 2012. Used by permission of Tyndale House Publishers, Inc., Wheaton, Illinois 60189. All rights reserved.

Director of Publications: David W. Ray
Managing Editor of Publications: Lance Colkmire
Editorial Assistant: Tammy Hatfield
Copy Editor: Esther Metaxas
Graphic Design and Layout: Michael McDonald

ISBN: 978-1-64288-080-9

Pathway

Copyright © 2019 by Pathway Press
1080 Montgomery Avenue
Cleveland, Tennessee 37311

All rights reserved. No part of this publication may be reproduced or transmitted in any form or by any means, electronic or mechanical, including photocopying, recording, or otherwise, or by any information storage or retrieval system, without the permission in writing from the publisher. Please direct inquiries to Pathway Press, 1080 Montgomery Avenue, Cleveland, TN 37311.

Visit *www.pathwaypress.org* for more information.

DEDICATION

With deepest gratitude to our Lord for
His patience with me
and the faithfulness of His Word;
with all my love to all of my family:
To my wonderful wife, Jan;
Bo, Jen, Natalie, and Julia;
Justin (and Jack);
Dad, Mom, Tom, Charla, Crystal, Chad;
and so many more.
And with deep appreciation to the
congregation of Praise Cathedral who
exemplify all I want to be in Christ!

—Pastor J

CONTENTS

ACKNOWLEDGMENTS 9

1. *Jesus Said:*
   "HAVE FAITH IN GOD" 11

2. *Jesus Said:*
   "YOU MUST BE BORN AGAIN" 25

3. *Jesus Said:*
   "BECOME LIKE A CHILD" 39

4. *Jesus Said:*
   "YOU MUST FORGIVE" 53

5. *Jesus Said:*
   "DO NOT WORRY ABOUT IT" 73

6. *Jesus Said:*
   "WHO TOUCHED ME?" 89

7. *Jesus Said:*
   "THE PROBLEM IS OUR HEART" 105

8. *Jesus Said:*
   "IF THESE ROCKS COULD TALK!" 121

9. *Jesus Said:*
   "I AM ALIVE" 131

10. *Jesus Said:*
    "WHAT IF . . . ?"...........................145

Acknowledgments

Oswald Chambers writes of the simplicity of Jesus' words and how difficult it is for our generation to accept them as such. Inspired by that thought, this book contains a series of sermons preached at Praise Cathedral, simply titled "Jesus Said."

I pray that these messages may speak to you and invite you to take them, perfect them, and use them to glorify our Lord.

"Jesus Said...
HAVE FAITH IN GOD"

Now the next day, when they had come out from Bethany, He was hungry. And seeing from afar a fig tree having leaves, He went to see if perhaps He would find something on it. When He came to it, He found nothing but leaves, for it was not the season for figs. In response Jesus said to it, "Let no one eat fruit from you ever again." And His disciples heard it. . . . Now in the morning, as they passed by, they saw the fig tree dried up from the roots. And Peter, remembering, said to Him, "Rabbi, look! The fig tree which You cursed has withered away." So Jesus answered and said to them, "Have faith in God. For assuredly, I say to you, whoever says to this mountain, 'Be removed and be cast into the sea,' and does not doubt in his heart, but believes that those things he says will be done, he will have whatever he says. Therefore I say to you, whatever things you ask when you pray, believe that you receive them, and you will have them" (Mark 11:12-14, 20-24).

Jesus Said...

I find it humorous when I consider the many difficult, and sometimes dangerous, circumstances in which Jesus was consistently placing His disciples. He was continually leading them into unique and challenging situations. From the disciples' point of view, I have little doubt that whatever situation they found themselves in, it was not amusing. But step back and consider the following: Twice when we read about the disciples getting in a boat, it nearly sank! On one of those occasions, Jesus did not even get in the boat with them, yet He sent them directly into a storm. After this, we might expect them to say, in essence, "Forget the boat. Next time, let's walk."

On one occasion, Jesus took His disciples into a graveyard where a demon-possessed person was known to live. Jesus knew some people hated both Him and His disciples—their hatred being so thick that they desired to kill Jesus—yet He would carry His disciples directly to where those people were.

Jesus knew the Jews hated the Samaritans, and He knew His disciples were Jews; but where did Jesus have to go in John 4? Right through Samaria! He waits until Lazarus has been dead four days, and then He says, "Now let's go help him."

He takes a large multitude of people on a three-day journey into the wilderness where He teaches them for many hours. He keeps them in the wilderness until all their supplies are exhausted. The disciples then look at Him and say, in essence, "Lord, this is good teaching, but we're a long way from the Waffle House, and we're out of food!" Once again the disciples are in the middle of an impossible situation, and Jesus tells them, "You feed them" (see Mark 6:37).

He was always putting them in hard places. I can picture the disciples sitting around the campfire after a long journey, talking about the challenges of the day. I am sure eye-rolling was taking place between them. There were probably times they looked at each other as if to say, *Can you believe what He is doing?*

For instance, when Jesus left Bethany to make His way to raise Lazarus from the dead, all of the disciples knew people in Lazarus' village were looking for a chance to kill Jesus. When Thomas realized where Jesus was leading them, he said, "OK, let's go be killed with Jesus" (see John 11:16).

It is easy for us to laugh when we read about those hard circumstances Jesus allowed His disciples to face. I am talking about the times their backs were against the wall—the times He would put them in places where all their provisions were gone, and they didn't have any idea what to do. There were days when Jesus put them in the presence of their enemies. Yes, difficult, painful, and awkward circumstances were a part of their discipleship journey. All of this seems so funny until I realize, He is doing the same thing with me.

Here is what I have discovered: All through our lives, God is continually leading us into uncomfortable situations and predicaments in which we would rather not be. We prefer the easy road, but He is not afraid of the hard road. We prefer smooth sailing. but He is not afraid of the storm.

Jesus Said...

A few years ago, my wife, Jan, and I took a last-minute cruise. At one point during the cruise, we were informed by the captain that the ship would be sailing through the remnant of Hurricane Danny. That captain was a liar! One of the many prayers I offered that afternoon was, "Lord, I will never talk about the disciples being afraid in the boat ever again—that time the storm hit, and the disciples in fear awoke You from Your nap. If I had been on that boat, Lord, I would have been the first one to wake You up!"

Whether we like it or not, Christ is always putting us in difficult and awkward places. The question is, Why? Why does He allow life to become so hard? Why must we go through dark seasons and experience hard times? Why does He not only allow it but often lead us in the path of adversity? I confess I do not have all the answers, but the Bible does.

Let us consider three truths that will not keep us from the storms but will, perhaps, keep us through the storms.

1. God often uses adversity to teach us about Himself.

I wish I could get this "God education" through another means. I wish that just by reading the Bible, I could be enlightened to the truth that He is the Healer, the Way-maker, the Deliverer, and the Provider. But it takes more than just reading about God's actions in the Bible to make them real to me. Truth does not become a reality to me until I experience it.

"Have Faith in God"

Jesus could have told the disciples that He had power over the wind, waves, and storms. However, those claims would have been unsubstantiated. Only by placing them on a sinking ship were the disciples able to know Jesus had the power to control the wind and waves by saying, "Peace, be still." I am sure when the winds and waves were crashing in on them, their preference would have been not to be there (I speak from experience). However, when the moment came, Jesus spoke the word, and the storm quieted. At that time, you can hear them giving thanks that He had sailed them through the storm to reach the other side. By allowing them to go through the storm, they found out they did not have to be afraid any longer. What eased their fear? Sitting among them was the One who was more powerful than the storm. They knew the One whom the wind and waves had to obey. They would never have experienced that truth if He had kept them from the storm. Jesus never said we wouldn't face storms, but He did say, "I will never leave you nor forsake you" (Heb. 13:5).

Had Jesus not put the disciples in circumstances where they did not have enough food, they would never have known that He can provide abundance out of lack. Many of us have been there—that place where we did not realize how ends were going to meet and we could not even find the ends to make them meet. That place where there is more month left at the end of the money. That place when everything within us has run out—our patience and our confidence have run out. That place where we felt dry and wasted away, yet suddenly comes a provision from the Lord—something out of nothing. It is in that place we would rather not be, that we realize we don't have to be afraid.

Nothing in sight? No worries. He doesn't need anything to make a way. He doesn't need anything to provide for my needs. Suddenly I realize being here, in these circumstances, is not an accident or coincidence. He brought me here! Not to destroy me, but to teach me.

Had Jesus not allowed His disciples to face demons, they would never have known He has all power and authority over demons. By waiting until Lazarus had died, Jesus showed His disciples that He is "the resurrection and the life" (John 11:25). Every crisis He placed them in was an opportunity to reveal something new and beautiful about the character of God.

In our crises and adversities, we need to learn to look for the revelation of God. Instead of saying, "Oh God, why me?" every time we face a crisis; we must learn to say, "Oh God, what are you showing me in this?" Jesus said time and again, "Have faith in God." He is saying, regardless of the circumstances, there is a God who cannot and will not fail. And, at the right moment, He will step in and reveal Himself in a way we have never seen Him before.

Sometimes it seems life leads us into a crisis. Other times we seem to get ourselves into a mess. There are also times when the people we are connected to bring the crisis into our lives (ask the sailors who let Jonah on their boat). No matter how we get into these situations, the truth remains: God is at His best when life is at its worst. It is in the lowest places in life that we will learn the most about Him.

I have learned more about God in the valleys of life than I have ever learned while listening to sermons or reading books. I have learned more about God through my storms than I have ever learned from hearing the testimonies of others. I can be glad, rejoice, and find strength in hearing the stories of how God was faithful to others. But I never really learned who He was or what He could do until He led me down that low road and took me through the dark place of trial. When I lived it, I discovered God is who He said He is.

2. In times of trouble, God develops character within us.

We see significant changes between the disciples at the beginning and when they matured (then referred to as the "apostles" in the Book of Acts), as it relates to their walk with the Lord.

Early on, these guys could not get along. They could not fight the devil because they were too busy fighting one another. They argued over such silly things as who was the greatest, who has the best seats at the table, and who should be closest to Jesus. They were self-centered, self-focused, and self-absorbed. When you get to the Book of Acts, they were willing to sell everything they had and give it to the poor. They regularly took beatings and imprisonment for the cause of the Gospel, and they were excited when they were considered worthy to suffer for Jesus Christ. What happened?

Jesus Said...

Pentecost and the indwelling of the Holy Spirit explains part of their metamorphosis. However, do not overlook that for over three years, Jesus had always put them in hard places where He was developing them into the people that He wanted them to be. He put them in hard places not because He wanted to break them, but to mold them into His image and likeness.

There are times when God will drive us to our knees merely to drive us to our knees, because He is more interested in our character than our comfort. He is more interested in the image of Christ inside of me than the glory of the life I seek around me. He leads me to difficult places because, at times, that it is the only way I will allow Him to take out of me what needs to be removed—bad attitudes, unhealthy relationships, poor spiritual disciplines, and so on.

There are some things within us that we don't give up easily. There are things we know we need to let go of but are unwilling to do so. So, what does God do? He allows us to get cornered, with no place to hide! The Apostle James said we should embrace these moments: "My brethren, count it all joy when you fall into various trials, knowing that the testing of your faith produces patience. But let patience have its perfect work, that you may be perfect and complete, lacking nothing" (James 1:2-4). He did not say to count it joy because testing produces miracles. He said to count it all joy because testing is building "Christ in you." When life is difficult, do not run from the difficulty, for God is at work inside of you.

I remember when a particular member of our church passed away, how my heart broke for the family. He was a retired minister who, by all appearances, was about to enjoy some years of reward for his labor. Suddenly, without warning, he was gone. His daughter and son-in-law had been part of our music ministry for many years. I worried about how the loss might impact them. Would they be discouraged, disappointed, or even disillusioned (I would)?

Amazingly after his passing, his daughter sang with greater anointing and passion than I have ever heard. Although the anointing was always there, something had changed in her having gone through the valley of heartbreak. The adverse circumstances did not do something *to them;* rather, the Lord had done something *in them.*

Why did James say we should "count it all joy" when we go through fiery trials, and why did Peter agree (1 Peter 1:6-7; 4:12-13)? Why count it joy? Because the testing of our faith produces endurance, and endurance can make us "mature and complete" (James 1:4 NIV). In my adversity, God is not trying to kill or destroy me, but He is trying to develop something within me that is more glorious than I could ever develop myself. That is why I must lift my eyes and say, "Here I am, Lord. Take the hammer and chip away so that I may be molded into the image of Christ."

3. The adversity we face today is building our faith for the adversity we will face tomorrow.

Jesus Said...

God knows exactly where the tipping point is. We look back at things we have been through and realize the challenges we faced then are helping us through the challenges we face now. For all of the crises and adversity Jesus allowed His disciples to meet, the greatest crisis was yet to come. What loomed on the horizon paled in comparison to sinking ships, lack of food, and screaming devils.

It is one thing for the ship to be sinking when Jesus is on the boat, and it is another thing for the ship to be sinking when He is off the boat. It is one thing to feed the multitudes when you have loaves and fishes, but what do you do when you do not have any supplies and Jesus is not there? It is one thing to stand beside Jesus when He calls Lazarus from the grave, but what will they do when it is Jesus' grave they are standing beside?

A few days before His crucifixion, Jesus saw a fig tree on the side of the road (Mark 11:12-24). It is bearing leaves as if it is bearing fruit, and Jesus is hungry. He walks up to the tree looking for fruit, but seeing no fruit on a leaf-bearing tree, He turns and curses the tree. The next day the disciples walk by, and they are amazed that the tree is dead! (This is one of those moments you want to ask the disciples what they thought was going to happen. This is the Man who speaks to the winds and waves, and they obey Him, and yet you are stunned that He cursed a tree and it died!) I am more amazed that the tree did not die the moment He cursed it.

The astonished disciples said, "Lord, the tree You cursed is dead!" You can almost hear Jesus say, "Come on, guys, look at everything you've seen. Consider the last three years. Haven't you learned anything?" Then Jesus said, "Have faith in God" (v. 22).

Those four simple words will revolutionize your life. Jesus would then go on to say if you have faith in God, you can expect to receive whatever you ask from God. You can speak to the mountain to move!

I believe Jesus knew the tree was bare. He knew it wasn't fig season. I think Jesus was showing the disciples something. He knew that in about a week, He would be crucified, and His crucifixion was going to be the most significant test of their faith. He was working today to prepare them for the adversity they would face tomorrow.

As I look back, things in my life that seemed so big and loomed so large, yet now in retrospect are nothing. The faith I gained in yesterday's battles enables me to face what looks so large in my life today. Whatever mountain we face, if we have faith in God, He can move the mountain.

Sometimes He doesn't move the mountain. I still must have faith in God. I have seen God move mountains suddenly and quickly; those moments are glorious! There are also those times He carried me over the mountain. It is in those moments that I had felt a little bit closer to Him than I did when He moved the mountain.

I have reached a point in my life where I have to pray: *Lord, I have faith in You, and if You decide to move the mountain, You can move it out of my way. However, if You don't move the mountain, I still have faith in You, and I know You will give me the strength, wisdom, and courage to overcome. I will get up every day and climb the mountain because I know You are climbing the mountain with me and Your presence will be near. Lord, I have learned to have faith in You in everything.*

Depending on what stage of life you are in, the mountains can loom so large. Young people face the mountains of academic pressure, peer pressure, the pressure to excel in extracurricular activities, and more. Parents, you do not have to put pressure on them, for the culture will do enough of that! To us who are older, we can tend to minimize the mountains of youth, but their mountains are just as significant to them as our mountains of finances, career, parenting, or whatever. So, to the kids who are worried about school, peer pressure, extracurricular endeavors, and whatever else is on the list . . . I say, *Have faith in God.* Write those words where you can see them daily: "Jesus said, 'Have faith in God.'" If it is important to you, it is important to God. If it is a big deal to you, it is a big deal to Him. If it is a mountain to you, it is a mountain to Him. You can have faith in God.

To the young adults who face the pressure of college and of "what's next" after college, have faith in God. It does not matter if you are wrestling with where to work or live, or how to get by and make ends meet, or even whom will you spend your life with, remember: "Have faith in God."

There is no mountain too large and no problem too small. He is Lord over them all, and we can trust Him. We can believe Him when we see Him, and we can trust Him when we don't. He promises He will never leave us, nor will He forsake us. God will guide you, and when you look back, you will see it was Him working in and through your life. Place your faith in God, and He will never fail you. God has given you that promise.

To those of us edging toward the latter years in life, we must have faith in God even when the spirit is willing but the flesh is weak. We think as we get older, the mountains will become easier to climb. However, they look as big now as they ever did, if not more significant. As the body continues to break down, our minds do not function like they used to, and that is just reality. We, too, need to hear Jesus' words, "Have faith in God!"

We must have faith in God, because the same God who took care of us in times past will take care of us today and tomorrow. The same God who got us through the early struggles will get us through the latter struggles. The same God who made a way last week will make a way next week and for all of time. Have faith in God!

Jesus Said...

SERMON STARTER
Jesus said: "Have faith in God."
Mark 11:12-14, 20-24

Throughout our lives, God continually leads us into uncomfortable situations and predicaments. We prefer the easy road, but He is not afraid of the hard road. We prefer smooth sailing, but He is not afraid of the storm.

1. **God often uses adversity to teach us about Himself.**
   A. Truth does not become a personal reality until I experience it.
   B. In my crisis and adversities, I need to learn to look for the revelation of God.
   C. God is at His best when life is at its worst.
2. **In times of trouble, God develops character within us.**
   A. God is more interested in your character than your comfort.
   B. When life gets hard, embrace it; God is doing something in you (James 1:2-5).
   C. In your adversity, God is trying to develop something within you that is more glorious than you could ever develop yourself.
3. **The adversity we face today is building our faith for the adversity we will face tomorrow.**
   A. God knows exactly where the tipping point is.
   B. The faith you gained in yesterday's battles enables you to face what looks so large in your life today.
   C. The same God who made a way last week will make a way next week and for all time.

2
"You Must Be Born Again"

There was a man of the Pharisees named Nicodemus, a ruler of the Jews. This man came to Jesus by night and said to Him, "Rabbi, we know that You are a teacher come from God; for no one can do these signs that You do unless God is with him." Jesus answered and said to him, "Most assuredly, I say to you, unless one is born again, he cannot see the kingdom of God" (John 3:1-3).

When you read the Gospels, it appears each writer addressed a different audience. Although they presented different themes, unity was not compromised.

Matthew appeared to address a primarily Jewish audience to convey Jesus was indeed the Messiah. *Mark* wrote his account to the church at large and is more abbreviated. *Luke,* a physician by trade, corresponded more to the human element, revealing the humanity of Christ.

John goes to great lengths to convey Jesus Christ is the Son of God. John emphasizes Jesus is God in human flesh. He is Deity who lived among us. John

Jesus Said...

declared, "In the beginning was the Word. . . . And the Word became flesh and dwelt among us, and we beheld His glory" (1:1, 14).

He recorded John the Baptist's great announcement, "Behold! The Lamb of God who takes away the sin of the world!" (v. 29). In chapter 2, the miracles begin, as Jesus turns the water into wine. Should there be any questions as to who Jesus claims to be, they are answered at the end of chapter 2, as Jesus cleansed the Temple and declared, "[This is] My Father's house" (v. 16). Jesus was not just another prophet or another teacher, but of certainty He is the Son of God.

Beginning in chapter 3, John gave the root of the Gospel. It is the foundation of his writing and all of the other Gospels. Verse 16 is the eternal passage of hope for every one of us: "For God so loved the world that He gave His only begotten Son, that whoever believes in Him should not perish but have everlasting life." This passage is from a conversation Jesus had with Nicodemus.

Nicodemus was "a man of the Pharisees . . . a ruler of the Jews" (v. 1). To be a Pharisee meant Nicodemus was a member of one of two major Jewish religious groups of his day, the other being the Sadducees. Think of the difference this way: the Pharisees were the conservatives, and the Sadducees were the liberals.

As a Pharisee, Nicodemus was strict in his commitment to the Old Testament law and the oral law (traditions), passed down from Moses through Joshua, the elders, and the prophets.

"You Must Be Born Again"

He worshiped at the Temple and was knowledgeable of all the proper procedures and protocols. He was devoted to the old ways to the "enth degree." Nicodemus knew the routines, feasts, and the observances. No one would have to coach or prompt Nicodemus on how to live! Sadly, though he knew so much about God, it appears he never knew the God he had learned so much about. That is a scary place to be—knowing of God but not knowing Him in a personal way.

Nicodemus was no ordinary religious zealot. He sat on the prestigious council called the *Sanhedrin*. His voice carried weight and influence, as we will see later in John's Gospel. The people of his community would listen to what Nicodemus had to say. In today's terminology, we would say Nicodemus had "gravitas." Nicodemus' query of Jesus with questions about eternal life revealed something significant: for all of his religious accomplishments, zeal, and performance, knowing he came to Jesus acknowledges he knew something was not right in his heart.

We must realize, like Nicodemus, it is not the externals that matter most. The externals should merely be reflections of something that has transpired internally. Nicodemus reminds us we can be fiercely religious and still be on a path to hell. His story helps us understand that even today, it is not about following the correct rules or using religious-sounding words. You may participate in all the religious activities, yet in and of themselves, all of your spiritual activity does not have the power to save your soul. Religious

Jesus Said...

activity cannot cleanse your heart. Religious activity cannot change you from what you once were to what you should be. We must realize that people can go to church every day of their lives and still go to hell.

That may sound harsh, especially in today's politically correct climate. The truth is that we are confused. What we know as "church" and "following Jesus" do not necessarily equate. I don't know how many times I have heard people say, "I've got to get back in church." While that is indeed an admirable goal, it does not save someone from hell. Your church relationship is not the issue of eternity. The bottom line is not church attendance, but where you stand with Him.

Don't get me wrong; it is right for you to attend church! But arguably, even the devil attends church (I can point to where he or she sits some Sundays!). It is good that you serve and give; it is good that you offer acts of worship and songs of praise. It is good that you do all of the things we deem as religious, just as Nicodemus did in his day. But these things will not give you eternal life. I doubt anyone participated in more religious activities than Nicodemus, yet he still knew something was missing in his life.

The question remains: Have you experienced new birth through Jesus Christ? Has He washed you of all your sins? Although you may never get to church again (serve, sing, or do any of the church things again as a part of your natural life), if you know Jesus Christ as your Lord and Savior, this new birth gives you the right to claim eternal life. The Apostle Paul declared, "Not by works of righteousness which we have done, but according to his mercy he saved us, by the washing of regeneration, and renewing of the Holy Ghost; which he shed on us abundantly through Jesus Christ our Saviour; that being justified by his grace, we should be made heirs according to the hope of eternal life" (Titus 3:5-7 KJV).

To get to the root of Nicodemus' problem, we need to consider John's first reference to him in 3:1: "There was a man." Do you see the problem? He, like all of us, was born into a human condition of being lost and estranged from God. Like Nicodemus, we are all born into a sinful state, controlled by a sinful nature that constantly wars against the image of God. As beautiful and innocent as babies are, the reality is they are born into sin, with a sinful nature. No, they have not committed "acts of sin," but they will. This is not an indictment on the child; it is the reality of humanity. Given time, the sin nature we are born with rises up and gives birth to sin in every one of us, no exceptions. Tragically, none of us has the power to conquer our sinful nature and free ourselves from this condition.

Andrew Murray is one of my favorite writers. In his masterpiece titled *Humility*, he says we fail to realize "the power that Satan brought from hell, and cast into man's life, is working daily, hourly, with mighty power throughout the world. Men suffer from it; they fear and fight and flee it; and yet they know not whence it comes, whence it has its terrible supremacy. No wonder they do not know where or how it is to be overcome."

Jesus Said...

We have a sin problem, and until we acknowledge that truth, we are never going to get better. We are all like Nicodemus—in the middle of a spiritual war that we cannot win on our own.

John also indicated Nicodemus came to Jesus at night. Being in the presence of the Son of God made Nicodemus fully aware of his lack. He knew something had to change. He said, "I know You are of God because no one can do what You do unless they are of God" (see v. 2). Nicodemus saw in Jesus something he had long hoped religion would give him, yet it never did.

People should see in us enough of Christ that it makes them hungry for what we have. You may never preach a sermon or hand out a tract. It may be difficult for you to initiate a conversation in which you share your testimony. But in the normal interactions of life, people should be able to look at us and recognize something (Jesus) is within us that they don't have. And that should birth within them a hunger!

Nicodemus saw something different in Jesus and inquired with the essential issue of how he could know God like Jesus knows God. Jesus said, "You must be born again" (v. 7; also see vv. 3, 5-6). You cannot fix yourself. Your mom and dad could not fix you. Your mother may have tried to love you into being good, and your father may have wanted to discipline you into being good, but that did not work. You must be born again!

Not only can you not fix yourself, you cannot fix other people. We live in a lost and dying world, and we cannot fix it. We can help it, but we cannot fix it. I appreciate church programs, ministries, civic organizations, and counselors that make it their mission to help people. It is a great blessing to have these resources available to us. While these programs and resources have their merits, they can never replace the born-again experience with Jesus Christ.

Jesus told Nicodemus he was born of flesh, and "that which is born of the flesh is flesh" (v. 6). Just as Satan cannot cast out Satan, the sinful cannot cast out sin. The flesh can only give birth to fleshly things, but when the Spirit gives the new birth, there is life. The Spirit of God enters the inner man and awakens the part of man that was dead—the part that died in the Garden when the first sin was committed. The Holy Spirit, through the shed blood of Jesus Christ, baptizes the believer into Christ, and suddenly an explosion of life erupts within the newborn believer. There is an eruption of joy unspeakable and full of glory. Previously blank faces are suddenly illuminated with glory and a smile of contentment they cannot contain. It is here (in the new birth) that people notice something has changed; something beyond anything of earth; but by the Spirit, we are born again! There are three key areas I would like to point out from Nicodemus' encounter with Jesus.

1. Nicodemus acknowledged his condition.

The fact that Nicodemus came to Jesus implies he knew something was not right. If Nicodemus had been satisfied with what the Pharisee experience had given him, he would have never looked for something else.

Jesus Said...

Until we acknowledge the dissatisfaction of our lost condition, there can never be a cleansing change within us. Isaiah had to acknowledge, "I am a man of unclean lips, and I dwell [among unclean people]" before the Lord could ever use him (see Isa. 6:5).

Consider the encounter Simon Peter had with Christ when he fell on his knees and said, "[Lord], depart from me, for I am a sinful man" (Luke 5:8). We have to own the truth that we are by nature sinful, separated from God, and our nature is bent toward sin. There is a sinful war within us, and this is why our mouth will say things, and while the words are coming out, your brain says, "Why are you saying that?" Paul taught that sin itself lies within our flesh (see Col. 3:2-11). Thus, our issue is not what has happened "to us," but what has not happened "within us." Until there is an acknowledgment, there will never be cleansing.

2. Nicodemus' acknowledgment led to his confession.

He confessed his inadequacies compared to what he saw in Christ. He acknowledged religion had not worked for him, and what he saw in Christ was what he had been wanting.

There is no cleansing and no new birth without sorrowful confession of our condition. The great men and women of Scripture would often confess they were wretched and hopeless without God. David was a man after God's own heart, but when you consider the totality of his story, in many ways he was a pretty sorry guy. From a moral perspective, some would consider King Saul was a much better man than David. However, Saul would never confess his sin. Saul denied to the prophet Samuel that he had been disobedient to God, while David pleaded to God, "Against You, You only, have I sinned. . . . Create in me a clean heart, O God, and renew a steadfast spirit within me" (Ps. 51:4, 10).

We will never get better until we sincerely confess we are lost and broken and this sin nature exists within us. We must also be willing to confess only Christ can redeem us. Jesus Christ was the One sent to recover, redeem, and return that which was lost. You may have tried everything; you may have read books, attended meetings and seminars, watched videos, and everything you can get your hands on to conquer the nature within you and the condition of your soul. You must realize your only hope is in Christ and kneel before Him. Admit your brokenness before Christ and confess only He has the power to change you.

3. Nicodemus' confession led to his repentance.

Repentance is the definitive turn in your life from going the wrong direction, making a 180-degree turn, and going the right direction. The beautiful picture John laid out in this story of Nicodemus is this: We see him acknowledge God and confess his lack, and then the work of repentance begins to take hold.

No, Nicodemus did not leave this encounter walking on water. John does not even report he made a decision for Christ that night. But the implication is,

Jesus Said...

Nicodemus started on a new path that night. Like many of us who have been born again, Nicodemus did not have it all figured out, and there were probably some things he still struggled with for a while. He seems to have started his walk with the Lord, still needing a lot of work.

Did the encounter with Jesus make a difference in Nicodemus? He is seen two more times again in John's Gospel. First, in 7:50-52, as accusations rise against Jesus, it is Nicodemus who stands before the whole counsel and intervenes. He says, "We can't condemn him without a trial" (see v. 51). Here is Nicodemus standing before his peers, daring to defend Jesus! It is evident God was working in Nicodemus.

In 19:39-40, we see him again. The people have condemned and crucified Jesus. The Bible says, "Nicodemus, who at first came to Jesus by night, also came, bringing a mixture of myrrh and aloes, about a hundred pounds. Then they took the body of Jesus, and bound it in strips of linen with the spices, as the custom of the Jews is to bury." It has taken some time, but now Nicodemus is publicly testifying of His affection for Christ!

Here is a news flash for many of us. We did not get to the place we are in Christ overnight, but we saw something in Christ that we could not escape. Maybe we tried to keep things normal like Nicodemus, but Jesus just kept showing up! Then, finally, unashamed and without embarrassment, there came that moment when we declared, "Jesus is Lord." It is simple; it is free; it is God's gift to us—eternal life. All we must do is acknowledge our need and accept God's gift. We acknowledge our condition and let Christ come in and give us life, hope, and cleansing through the blood He shed for us.

One day I was near a hospital when I received a call that a family there needed a minister. As far as I knew, I had never met this family before. They were all gathered in the emergency room, as a member of the family had tragically and suddenly passed away (under questionable circumstances).

I began to pray and console them through the Word; I did my best to be a pastor to them. There are some situations we find ourselves in, and we know we don't have the words to change anything, so we pray the presence of God will move in the situation. As I was meeting the family members and praying, suddenly I was tapped on the shoulder. There stood a lady I didn't know; nor did I know how she was connected to the family. She instantly instructed me to tell the family their loved one was in heaven. I said, "Ma'am, I must tell you that I don't make that decision. I don't give eternal life. That is a decision between that person and God."

Moms and dads cannot make that decision for their children. Wives cannot make that decision for their husbands. Pastors cannot make it for anyone but themselves. So, here is the question: Do you have the hope of eternal life? Have you been born again? Today, you can know Jesus Christ has saved you from your sins. If you turn to Christ, He will not reject you; He will welcome you with open arms.

Jesus Said...

Pray this prayer:

Lord Jesus, I'm broken. The problem is not my environment nor my family or friends. It's me, and what's inside of me, and I acknowledge I am broken.

Lord. I confess my sinful condition and that you are the Christ, the Son of the living God. Forgive me today, Lord. Create in me a clean heart and renew a right spirit within me. Let me breathe the fresh air of new birth and know You are alive in me.

I receive You today as my Savior and Lord.

SERMON STARTER

Jesus said: "You must be born again."
John 3:1-21

John 3:16 is the everlasting promise of hope for every one of us. This scripture is from a conversation Jesus had with a Pharisee named Nicodemus. We see three key areas from Nicodemus' encounter with Jesus.

1. **His encounter with Jesus led to an acknowledgment.**
   A. Nicodemus' coming to Jesus implies he knew something was not right.
   B. Until we acknowledge the dissatisfaction of our lost condition, there can never be a cleansing change within us.
   C. Our issue is not what has happened "to us" but what has not happened "within us."

2. **His acknowledgment led to his confession.**
   A. He confessed his inadequacies compared to what he saw in Christ.
   B. There is no cleansing or new birth without sorrowful confession of our condition.
   C. We must be willing to confess that only Christ can redeem us.

3. **His confession led to his repentance.**
   A. *Repentance* is making a 180-degree turn and moving in the right direction.
   B. Nicodemus did not have it all figured out, and there were probably some things he still struggled with for a while.
   C. How do we know God was working in Nicodemus (see John 7:50-52; 19:39)?

3
"Jesus Said...
BECOME LIKE A CHILD"

At that time the disciples came to Jesus, saying, "Who then is greatest in the kingdom of heaven?" Then Jesus called a little child to Him, set him in the midst of them, and said, "Assuredly, I say to you, unless you are converted and become as little children, you will by no means enter the kingdom of heaven. Therefore whoever humbles himself as this little child is the greatest in the kingdom of heaven" (Matt. 18:1-4).

This thing called *life* is a vicious, confusing cycle. Think about it. We are celebrated as babies. We are adored as toddlers. Even in those early-elementary years when we lose those first two teeth on the bottom row, and we can't say words with the letter "s" very well, we often hear, "You are just the cutest thing that has ever been!"

Then, somewhere between second grade and fifteen years of age, something horrible happens. For some reason, the people who used to celebrate and adore you seem to grow weary of you. This is frustrating because when you are fifteen, you "know everything" and have

Jesus Said...

life completely figured out. If you were ever going to be celebrated, surely this would be the time!

Frustration increases because in the early days we heard phrases like, "I hope you never grow up" and "You will always be my baby!" Then, somewhere around puberty, we start to be interrogated with questions like, "When are you going to grow up?" and "When are you going to leave this house?"

The irony is when an adult, generally with fire coming out of their eyes, demands to know, "When are you going to grow up and be like me?" The teenager is thinking, *Why would I want to be like you? You're the one with the ulcer, and you're the one on Prozac!"* When we think of it in those terms, inviting a teenager to grow up is not an attractive proposition.

In reading Matthew 18:1-4, it appears there is a discussion between Jesus and His disciples regarding the kingdom of heaven. The disciples ask, "Who then is greatest in the kingdom of heaven?" (v. 1). They saw Christ's kingdom as for adults only, and that somehow you have to "adult" your way into His kingdom.

The question they ask appears to be a very adult question. That is, until Jesus bursts their theology bubble by declaring, "Unless you change and become like little children, you will never enter the kingdom of heaven" (v. 3 NIV). Jesus then added, "Whoever takes the lowly position of this child [the one Jesus had placed before them] is the greatest in the kingdom of heaven" (v. 4 NIV). Suddenly, we are brought to the reality that maybe the disciples got this Kingdom thing all wrong. And perhaps we today are still getting this Kingdom thing wrong.

The statement of Jesus was not a call to abandon maturity and behave like children. That would not be an accurate reflection of Kingdom living, although immaturity does seem to be a common theme among some believers. Let us look briefly at the kingdom of heaven, and strive to understand what is at stake.

The Bible teaches there is a physical place God is preparing for His children (John 14:1-3). There is coming a day when He will come for His children. He will carry us away into this place called heaven, where there is no more sickness nor pain. There will be no more death, and all the former things will pass away. So, yes, there is this physical kingdom of heaven.

There is also another realm of Christ's kingdom. The word *kingdom* translates to "the reign or rule of God." The kingdom of heaven is a physical place, but it is also a state of existence in which you and I are to live in now. We are to live under the rule and reign of God today, not just some far-off time in the future. Jesus said the Kingdom has come among us, now!

In Luke 17:21, Jesus declared, "Nor will they say, 'See here!' or 'See there!' For indeed, the kingdom of God is within you." I believe Jesus is referencing both to the kingdom of heaven that is to come and His kingdom that we are living in now. Paul said we are already seated in "heavenly places in Christ Jesus" (Eph. 2:6); thus, Kingdom living doesn't begin when we get to heaven, it starts now!

Jesus Said...

In Romans 14:17 Paul wrote, "For the kingdom of God is not eating and drinking, but righteousness and peace and joy in the Holy Spirit." That means the Kingdom is righteousness *now*, peace *now*, and joy in the Holy Spirit *now*. The effect of Kingdom living is righteousness, joy, and peace *now*!

Sadly, it does not appear the modern church has very much righteousness, peace, and joy in the Holy Spirit. What is wrong? Perhaps we have missed a great truth. We say we want to be right with God; we want to have the peace of God; and, we want to have the joy of God. Jesus implied the full dispensation of the Kingdom would never be exhibited in our lives unless we become like a child. Unless you become like a child, the rule and reign of God cannot come into your life.

Jesus did not say we should act like a child. Instead, our state of existence is being children of God in close relationship with our heavenly Father. So, we should have the mind-set of a child.

A small child is totally dependent. When a baby is born, if someone doesn't care for the baby, it will not survive. Someone must provide food, clothing, warmth, and shelter for the baby to not only survive but also to grow. Someone must provide instruction for the essential functions of life (walking, talking, etc.).

Dangers to avoid must be instilled into children because they are naïve and tend to trust everything. Children are completely dependent. God wants His children to be totally dependent on Him, which is how we enter into Kingdom living.

The Kingdom demand for dependence puts us in an internal conflict. Why? Because there is something within each of us that craves independence. The allure of adulthood is that we will be independent. That is why when you tell your teenager, "There are some things you cannot do until you grow up," he or she is thinking, *I can't wait to grow up so I can get out of here!* They believe when they are grown and out on their own, their independence means they will not have to follow anyone's rules. They think, *I can sleep as late as I want; I can wear the clothes I want to wear; and I can go where I want to go.* The desire to be independent is coded into our DNA.

However, independence comes with a price. The price of independence is responsibility. When you live independently, you are also responsible for the choices you make and the outcome those choices bring, good and bad.

Amazingly, here is God's offer: Accept the role of the child. Live in absolute dependence on God, and He will supply your every need. The Lord promises we will never have to worry or be afraid. Why? We have a loving heavenly Father who will look out for our well-being. The Lord is offering to take the worry, stress, and anxiety, in exchange for His righteousness, peace, and joy. That is what living as His children looks like, and this is a good deal!

Jesus not only said to convert and become like children, or you will not enter the kingdom of God, but He also declared the one who is greatest among us is the

Jesus Said...

one who is the humblest. He links *humility* as the portal by which the kingdom of God is displayed in our life!

Andrew Murray said, "Humility, the place of entire dependence on God, is, from the very nature of things, the first duty and the highest virtue of the creature, and the root of every virtue."

Here is the revelation: *This is where God wants me. He wants me living in humble, obedient dependence on Him.* Here is the beauty of this: *When I am living in humble, obedient, dependence on Him, the outcome of my life rests as His responsibility, not mine!*

If I choose to live independently, I must be responsible to make things go my way. However, if I come to my Father like a child; if I wake up and live in humble, obedient dependence, then every day I am assured my heavenly Father will take care of me. He will provide for my needs, watch out for me, and prepare the way for me; then I can rest in Him. Again, here is where we see the disposition of the Kingdom: righteousness, joy, and peace.

Let us look at three dimensions of the childlike life.

1. Children are a reflection of their environment.

If you want to know what the home is like, watch the child. Children say what they hear their parents say, do what they see their parents do, and interact as they see their parents interact. We think they are not listening when they are engaged in other activities (like coloring or playing with toys), but they hear every word. Not only do they listen to what you say, but they also understand the intonation of your voice.

Has your child said something, and you wonder, *Where did they hear that?* Chances are, they heard it at home! They are merely reflecting their environment. Their reaction to life is a reflection of how you respond to life. They come as blank pages, and you are writing on them every day. If you live nervously, they will live nervously. If you are easily provoked, they will become easily provoked. Every child is a reflection of the environment in which they live.

When we truly become like a child in the kingdom of heaven, we will naturally become a reflection of our heavenly Father in everything we do and say. Jesus is calling us to be children who live in such a close relationship with our heavenly Father that every day of our life, we are living reflections of Him. We are to be living reflections of our Lord Jesus Christ in every interaction of our lives. That means on the job, on our commute, at home, in the church. Yes, this includes the mundane tasks of life.

Jesus said He was a living reflection of His Father. In humble submissiveness, He declared, "The Son can do nothing of Himself, but what He sees the Father do; for whatever He does, the Son also does in like manner" (John 5:19). He so reflected His Father that He openly declared, "He who has seen Me has seen the Father" (14:9). Perpetual reflection of the image of God is to be our life!

Jesus Said...

When I was a young child, my mother retells the story of a time when my father was a postman in the Brandon Mill Community just outside of Greenville, South Carolina. He would park his postal truck and walk most of his route through the streets of the community. One afternoon my mother and I went to a store in the area, and a lady we had never met approached my mother and said, "This has to be my postman's son."

My mother replied, "Where do you live?" The lady replied, "Brandon Mill," and my mother said, "You are correct; your postman is his father." The lady went on talking about how much my father and I looked alike.

That story stands as an example of how we should live so close to our heavenly Father that others can see us and know we are His children. We should aim to be so close to Him that everywhere we go, people will say, "You must be a child of the Father!" People watch us as we go through the highs and lows of life. Through our responses, let us show we are children of the King.

Remember, children are a reflection of their environment. If we want to reflect our Father, then we must live in His presence.

2. Children are never shy to ask.

Children will ask any question, and they will ask for anything they want! When something catches the eye of a child, they will ask for it without giving any regard to the object's value or the person to whom the object belongs. If you have had children, you probably had the same conversation more than once, especially when you visited someone's house: "When we get there, do not ask for anything!" Of course, they still do, because they are still children.

One of the problems with growing up is we tend to quit asking for things. Somewhere, over time, it becomes ingrained in our minds that we are not supposed to ask for anything. Instead, we are supposed to make our way; that is what adults do. Jesus clearly taught: "Ask, and it will be given to you; seek, and you will find; knock, and [the door] will be opened to you. For everyone who asks receives; and he who seeks finds, and to him who knocks [the door] will be opened" (Matt. 7:7-8).

Listen to what Jesus said. God, your Father, is not afraid for you to ask! What a comfort to know that God is not scared for us to ask. He is not afraid to say no when that is the best answer, but He is also not afraid for you to ask. In the Kingdom, asking is the path for receiving.

As I was preparing this series of message, I caught myself fussing (within myself) over some things going on around me. This continued for some time until, finally, the Holy Spirit quickened my heart and said, "Why don't you ask Me to help you with that situation?"

I had no real answers other than, "I don't know." So, I asked. I prayed about it and asked for Him to help me in the situation that was irritating me. Suddenly, my troubled mind was covered in peace.

Jesus Said...

Wouldn't it be something for us to get to heaven and discover dispensations of joy, love, peace, and laughter that were available for us, and our Father was prepared to give us, but because we never asked we never received? Children are not afraid to ask, nor should we be afraid. We have a heavenly Father who invites us to ask, and He is not afraid to give. He loves to give!

3. Children are trusting.

Children are the most straightforward and purest form of trust we can ever know. When you tell a child a fantastic tale, as farfetched as it may seem, because you told them, they believe! Remember when your kids had that first loose tooth on the bottom row? Every time you tried to pull that wiggly tooth, they would resist for fear of possible pain. Then, you told them the story about the tooth fairy. Suddenly, they believed though this process may be initially painful, the reward that awaits them makes it all worthwhile. Because you said so, they trusted the prize would be worth the pain. *A child will take you at your word, and they will hold you to your word.*

When Jesus said unless we change and become like a child, He is permitting us to hold Him to His Word. We can trust that while life may have times of difficulty, the reward that awaits us will far outshine the pain. As children, with complete trust, we are invited to hold God to His Word in every circumstance we face.

I find great freedom when I think about how children live. I do not see many children who deal with

"Become Like a Child"

ulcers; it is an adult thing. Generally, kids do not have nervous breakdowns; that too is an adult thing. Now I am thinking this "convert and become like a child" thing sounds pretty good!

A sweet grandmother in our congregation passed away recently. The memorial service was held at the church, and I observed as members of the family expressed grief in various ways, but it was the grief of one of the grandchildren that especially caught my eye. She was about nine years old, and she was crushed at the loss of her grandmother. When the family made their way into the church, and as she sat down on the front pew, you could see the grief tormenting her little heart. Her eyes filled with tears as she buried her head in her mother's shoulder. Throughout the entire service, this precious little girl was so sad.

We made our way to the cemetery where we would commit the body back to the earth. Prompted by the Holy Spirit, I did not talk to the adults at the grave. Instead, I spoke of burial and resurrection with the children in mind. I told them that their grandmother was not here in this grave. Her body is here, but her soul is in heaven with Jesus. We know to be absent from the body is to be present with the Lord. I said that is where Grandma is, and one day she will return with the Lord, and we all will be together again.

After the service concluded, I stood to the side and spoke to the girl's father. Both of us looked toward a distant tree and watched as the little girl stood there alone. We noticed she was looking toward the grave,

Jesus Said...

and having a conversation with no one in particular. Her little lips were moving, and her dad said, "She is in her own world."

Later that evening, her dad asked her about what she was saying, and to whom was she talking. The little girl replied she was telling her grandmother how she hated leaving her body in the ground, but she knew she was not there but was really with the Lord. Then the girl promised Grandma that she was going to live for Jesus so she could see her one day in heaven. This same child that I saw sobbing in her mother's arms smiled and said to her father, "Daddy, it's OK."

Unless we convert and become like a child, we cannot see the kingdom of heaven. The problem with grown-ups is that too often we let what we know in our head blind the faith that is supposed to be in our heart.

Sermon Starter
Jesus said: "Become like a child"
Matthew 18:1-4

The kingdom of heaven is a literal place, but it is also a state of existence in which you and I are to live in now. We are to live under the rule and reign of God today, not just some far-off time in the future. Jesus said the Kingdom has come among us *now*.

1. **Children are a reflection of their environment.**
   - **A.** Children say what they hear their parents say; they do what they see their parents do.
   - **B.** When we truly become like a child in the kingdom of heaven, we will become a reflection of our heavenly Father.
   - **C.** Perpetual reflection of the image of God is to be our life.
2. **Children are never shy to ask.**
   - **A.** God, your Father, is not afraid for us to ask (Matt. 7:7-11).
   - **B.** In the Kingdom, asking is the path for receiving.
   - **C.** We have a heavenly Father who is not afraid for us to ask, and He is not afraid to give. He loves to give.
3. **Children are trusting**.
   - **A.** We are invited to hold God to His Word.
   - **B.** We can trust that while life may have times of difficulty, the reward that awaits us will far outshine the pain.
   - **C.** Unless we convert and become like a child, we cannot see the kingdom of heaven.

"*Therefore, the kingdom of heaven is like a certain king who wanted to settle accounts with his servants. And when he had begun to settle accounts, one was brought to him who owed him ten thousand talents. But as he was not able to pay, his master commanded that he be sold, with his wife and children and all that he had, and that payment be made. The servant therefore fell down before him, saying, 'Master, have patience with me, and I will pay you all.' Then the master of that servant was moved with compassion, released him, and forgave him the debt.*

"*But that servant went out and found one of his fellow servants who owed him a hundred denarii; and he laid hands on him and took him by the throat, saying, 'Pay me what you owe!' So his fellow servant fell down at his feet and begged him, saying, "Have patience with me, and I will pay you all." And he would not, but went and threw him into prison till he should pay the debt. So when his fellow servants saw what had been done, they were very grieved, and came and told their master all that had been done. Then his master, after he had called him, said to him, 'You wicked servant! I forgave you all that debt because you begged me. Should you not also have had compassion on your fellow servant, just as I had pity on you?' And his master was angry, and delivered him to the torturers until he should pay all that was due to him.*

"So My heavenly Father also will do to you if each of you, from his heart, does not forgive his brother his trespasses" (Matt. 18:23-35).

When you have been in church long enough, you know the script. You know the terminology so well it becomes empty rhetoric. I spend enough time in church meetings and in reading the press of the church that I honestly have become frustrated. It seems I hear the same story, over and over. Nothing ever changes.

For instance, take the worship style. It doesn't matter if your preferred style is contemporary or traditional; both sides seem to adhere to their predictable script. For the contemporaries, it becomes about changing the stage every six weeks and going with a new theme or sermon series. We will have to get new banners and, of course, we will have to have matching T-shirts to give away. That is not a condemnation; I am just pointing out how easily we become scripted.

For the traditionalists, it is about not changing anything . . . ever. Don't even ask! The same songs are sung, and the same old routines are observed. You could go into a coma for ten years, recover, and return to church and feel that you haven't missed a Sunday!

"YOU MUST FORGIVE"

Even the same style of sermon is preached, in the same method, and concludes with the same dramatic finish.

Somewhere in this process, we have taken the simple Gospel and made it complicated. That has birthed a hunger within me to find out what Jesus said. I find myself at gatherings hearing people's opinions, and I want to stand up and shout out, "Just tell me what Jesus said!" That's all I need to know.

It is with this thought in mind that I bring you this statement: *Jesus said you have to forgive.* I am sure you have heard this before. However, I am equally sure you need to listen to it again. You cannot live a day without someone offending you or without you hurting someone else. Therefore, we need to constantly give forgiveness, as well as receive forgiveness. At some point in your day, you will need both sides of the forgiveness coin.

The parable in Matthew 18 is a result of Simon Peter asking, "How many times a day must I forgive my brother? Seven times?" (see v. 21). The implication is that Simon Peter realizes that every day, someone offends him. It is virtually impossible to make it through a single day without someone offending you. If a person had one day that they didn't interact with any other human being, they would still be offended that no one called or tried to get in contact with them.

Here we find a universal principle that affects everyone—offenses will come. Jesus said, "It is impossible that no offenses should come, but woe to him through whom they do come!" (Luke 17:1).

Jesus Said...

One day between our morning services, having just preached about forgiveness, a man approached me and said: "I've been enjoying your sermons *lately*." Think about that for a minute—lately? The human part of me wanted to say, "Lately? I've been here for eighteen years!" Then the other side wanted to say, "Well, I've been trying to do better."

I knew the heart of what the gentleman meant, but the point is that the opportunity to be offended will come every day. Truthfully, we are the ones who decide whether we want to be offended or not. Like everything else in life, it is a choice we make. No one can force us to be offended!

I believe offenses fall into one of two categories:

First, there are real offenses. Real offenses are those circumstances when you are genuinely wronged. Someone may harm you; they may tell a lie about you or cheat on you. People can act in ways that wound you deeply, and because there is a cause, I deem these offenses "real." Our choir has a song they sing occasionally. It talks about being "lied about, cheated, talked about, and mistreated, rebuked and scorned, just as sure as you're born." The church gets all excited singing that song. Everyone will be standing, clapping, and even shouting as the song talks about being mistreated. Go figure!

Second, there are perceived offenses. These offenses are not the result of something that has occurred; rather, they stem from what is "perceived" to have occurred. For instance, you see some friends standing around

"You Must Forgive"

talking. When you walk up, they suddenly stop the conversation. In your mind, you assume they had to be saying negative things about you, or else why would they stop and just look at you? Your perception was that, because they stopped talking, the conversation had to be negative. Your perception of the event would never allow the possibility they could have been discussing your surprise birthday party, or buying you a gift! Perception minus facts can be a dangerous thing.

Living with perceived offenses is precisely where the enemy wants us to live. That is why the power of God must transform our mind (see Rom. 12:1-2). We have this thing called an *imagination* where we tend to set unrealistic expectations about people. When they don't live up to our expectations (and these are often expectations we have never told them about), we get offended if they fall short of our perceptions (see 2 Cor. 10:3-6).

My mother worked for many years at an air-conditioning company. One day my dad picked up my mom from work, and when she got in the car, she began speaking in a very angry tone. She wasted no time announcing, "Do you know what the devil told me today?"

My dad was shocked, and said, "No, what?"

She quickly quipped, "The devil told me that you don't love me!"

For those who don't know my dad, he has always been a sharp fellow with a quick wit. He replied just as quickly, "Why that lying rascal!"

Jesus Said...

His response instantly brought a smile of relief to Mom's face. But then Dad finished his thought: "He promised me he wouldn't tell you!"

The devil will do anything he can to get it in your mind that someone doesn't like you, someone is against you, or someone has done you wrong. Here is the danger with perceived offenses: they can be just as powerful as real transgressions. Perceived offenses carry just as much hurt and damage as real offenses. Jesus teaches that it does not matter if the offenses are real or perceived, there is only one remedy: *You must forgive!*

Understand that offenses are a trap of the devil, and it is a prison where he wants to incarcerate God's children. Offenses open the heart for the poison of resentment to develop and the root of bitterness to take place. The writer of Hebrews instructs us to pluck out the "poisonous root of bitterness" (12:15 NLT) because it will poison your worship, your spirit, and even your conversations. Talk to someone with a bitter root in their life for three minutes, and you will know it immediately.

Jesus reveals the seriousness of offenses, teaching that they prevent true worship of God. Jesus said if you come into the house of the Lord and remember there is something between you and your brother or sister, you are to leave your gift at the altar and go first and be reconciled (Matt. 5:23-24). The implication is, we cannot rightly worship God in a vertical relationship if there are issues between us and others in our horizontal relationships.

In Jesus' parable in Matthew 18, the weight of offenses come to their highest level as Jesus says if you do not forgive others, it will prevent the grace of God from forgiving you. The notion of refusing to forgive is nothing to be played with or taken lightly. You must understand, the illusion of holding onto offenses is that you feel like you are putting the offender in prison, while you are the one sitting in the cell. We, the ones who are offended, struggling with forgiveness, are often the ones that can't sleep at night or can't enjoy a good meal. All the while, the other person (the one who offended us) can seem to go on through life unaffected (this also offends us!).

Perhaps this is what Jesus meant in verse 34: "And his master was angry, and delivered him to the torturers until he should pay all that was due to him." All too often, it is the person who holds to offenses that becomes the one who is tortured. The adage says it best: "Holding to offenses and grudges is like one man drinking poison, hoping the other person will die."

The issue is clear: Everyone will be offended. You can't run from it, because wherever you find people, offenses are going to occur. It doesn't matter where you work. You can quit a job today because you have been offended by someone. However, as soon as you find another job, you will at some point be offended there as well.

You will also live with people who will hurt you. Yes, at times people in your family will offend you. People in the church will offend you, no matter which church you attend.

Jesus Said...

I heard the story of a man who was shipwrecked. He was all alone on a deserted island. Finally, he was rescued. The rescuers were amazed to see that, over time, he had built three buildings on the island. When asked what the buildings were for, he replied, "The first one is where I live, and the next one is where I worship the Lord."

Someone asked about the third building, and he quickly replied: "That's where I used to attend church." Wherever you go in life, people will offend you, and the only way to learn to deal with that is to remember Jesus said, "You must forgive them."

We must bear in mind what Jesus did *not* say, because that can be as important as what He said.

1. Jesus did not say the offender is innocent.

Just because you forgive someone does not mean that person is not guilty of offenses. Neither does it mean offending parties are not responsible for their wrong. Many times, we struggle with forgiveness because we are afraid someone will get off scot-free. Forgiveness says because God has forgiven me, I can forgive you. If you struggle with that, consider the forgiveness of God is "freeing" forgiveness. Having been freed by God's forgiveness, we cannot let our unwillingness to forgive put us in prison. I cannot allow my destiny in Jesus Christ to be sidetracked because someone has done me wrong or let me down. Forgiving someone does not mean they are not guilty; it just means their offense will not imprison me.

The story of Joseph (Gen. 37—50) is often referenced when talking about forgiveness. Joseph was a young man when God revealed his destiny to him in two dreams. Joseph began sharing his dreams with his brothers, and they were resentful (and probably afraid). Instead of embracing what God was doing, the brothers sold young Joseph into slavery, and then pretended he had been killed by a wild animal. Everything his brothers did was wrong. Little did Joseph know that his troubles were just beginning.

Joseph ended up a slave in Potiphar's house, where Potiphar's wife sold Joseph out by lying about him. As a result of her lie, Joseph was thrown into prison. There, he met a cupbearer to Pharaoh, who assured Joseph that when he got out of prison, he would speak to Pharaoh on his behalf. As soon as the cupbearer was released, however, he forgot his promise, leaving Joseph to rot in jail.

If anyone had the right (from a human standpoint) to harbor resentment on multiple levels, it would be Joseph. If anyone had the right to become an embittered man, Joseph would be the prime candidate. However, he chose to live a life of forgiveness, and that forgiveness enabled God to take him from the pit to the palace. Joseph would not let real offenses keep him from God's destiny for his life. Concerning Joseph's time in prison, Genesis 39:23 says, "The Lord was with Joseph and gave him success in whatever he did" (NIV).

Jesus Said...

God does not bless a bitter heart, or an unforgiving heart. God said we cannot genuinely worship Him with an unforgiving heart. Thus, for the Lord to be with Joseph and give him prosperity in "whatever he did," it is obvious Joseph chose to live in forgiveness.

We may never know what people will do to us or say to us or about us. However, we have absolute power as to how we respond. Perhaps the most beautiful response in the Old Testament is when Joseph spoke to his brothers when they were reunited. Remember, their actions had created the turmoil in the first place. Joseph now had the power to destroy his brothers, should his heart be so inclined. Instead, we can hear the spirit of forgiveness coming from Joseph's heart: "Joseph said to them, 'Do not be afraid, for am I in the place of God? But as for you, you meant evil against me; but God meant it for good, in order to bring it about as it is this day, to save many people alive. Now therefore, do not be afraid; I will provide for you and your little ones.' And he comforted them and spoke kindly to them" (50:19-21). Joseph's words were not those of a bitter man. No! He chose to forgive.

2. **Jesus did not say forgiving the offender means you do not have to be wary of him or her in the future.**

We can forgive today, but it does not mean we put ourselves in a position to be taken advantage of tomorrow. *Forgiveness is an issue of the heart, but it does not nullify using your head.*

"YOU MUST FORGIVE"

I can loan you my wife's car (you can't have mine), and you can wreck it. I can forgive you for wrecking it, but that does not mean I will loan you a car again tomorrow. You may be a lousy driver. Forgiving you of the accident is an issue of the heart, but that does not nullify using the wisdom of the head the next time you want to borrow her car.

Consequently, I may forgive you for breaking a promise yesterday, but that does not mean I will cling to a promise you make me tomorrow. In Luke 16, Jesus told the parable of a master who "commended" an unjust servant for being "shrewd" (v. 8). Here, the word *shrewd* translates as "uses good judgment."

If you are in business with someone and discover they are stealing from the business, forgiving them does not mean you have to go back into business with that person. Looking back at the story of Joseph, it is interesting that while he forgave his brothers, he never traveled with them again! (Yes, they traveled together to bury their father, but a caravan of Egyptians also accompanied them). Let that sink in a bit. His brothers show up and Joseph says, "You are forgiven"; and, paraphrasing the rest of the conversation, he says, "Now you go and live in Goshen, but I am going to stay right here."

I recall a time when a man thought he wanted to work for me. Every time he saw me, that was the focus of his conversation. Finally, the day arrived when the opportunity came. For new hires and transfers, our company mandated a ninety-day probationary period.

During this period, the employer or the employee could end the employment with no questions asked.

Sure enough, this new hire did not exactly make it the full ninety days. He discovered the *illusion* of working for me wasn't the *reality* of working for me. His leaving me put me in a bad spot, for I had gone out on a limb to hire him. But that is the way things go. Several years passed before our paths crossed again. When I saw him, I headed straight for him and embraced him. I asked him about how his life was transpiring. I genuinely harbored no bitter feelings about this individual. But I also know if he applied for a job to work for me again, I would never consider it! While forgiveness is a heart issue, it should never nullify level-headed judgment when making decisions tomorrow.

3. Jesus never said to forgive only when someone asks for it.

Some people may never ask for forgiveness. The more stunning reality is that some people may never know they have offended you. How could someone ask for forgiveness from you if they have never realized or understood they have hurt you? Forgiveness is not an act that must be pleaded for or earned. It is prideful to think someone must earn our forgiveness through some form of penance. Forgiveness is acknowledging that because Christ has forgiven us, we must forgive others.

Some people who have offended us will never have the opportunity to ask for our forgiveness. They may have already passed from this life, or they may be in a different physical location. In either case, there will be times people cannot or will not be able to ask you for your forgiveness. If you continue to choose to walk in resentment, the consequences can be tragic. Remember when you hold on to the offense, *you* are the one imprisoned, even though *you* are the one who holds the key to freedom. Releasing them from the offense, whether they have asked or not, actually releases you to live free.

Look at the parable where the king had decided to settle accounts. Jesus taught in the Sermon on the Mount that we should settle our accounts *quickly.* Allowing things to go unchecked is serious. Why? Because, whatever is not dealt with has the potential to fester, and it will eventually burst open and poison your inner self. The longer it rests in your heart, the greater the power it will exert over you. The more you talk to others about your offenses and how you were done wrong, the greater the offenses become in your mind. Each time you replay an offense, the larger it grows. An issue that started small and insignificant will bloom into something that can ruin your life and the lives of others. The irony is that things can grow so large and out of hand that, over time, you don't even remember the first offense!

When you refuse to deal with the issue at hand and allow it to settle in your life and grow, it can metamorphose into a monstrosity you could never have envisioned. So, Jesus said, "Settle matters quickly." He

Jesus Said...

added that when you are on your way to the judge or the meeting, settle the matter even before you get there.

In another place, Jesus instructs us on how we should settle matters quickly: He says to go to the offender privately (Matt. 18:15). You go to the person yourself; it is just you and the other person. *It is amazing how many things can be taken care of if we sit down and have a conversation.*

Remember the pattern: The longer you hold on to resentment, the bigger it grows in your mind, the deeper it settles in your heart, and the more it affects your life. *Settle it quickly.*

Please understand that an offended heart is going to affect more than just you. When the servant approaches the king about his massive debt, who does the king initially discuss putting into prison? He does not say he will imprison just the servant, but also the servant's wife and his children.

When you have an embittered heart, it affects more than you; it affects everyone around you. People with embittered hearts "snap" at people who had nothing to do with the issues that are causing their bitterness. Then the poison spreads. Bitter parents raise bitter children. Bitter spouses live in bitter houses. Kids will grow up being angry and offended, and they often do not even know why they are angry and offended. They think it is just the way their parents live. Your offense will affect more than you.

"YOU MUST FORGIVE"

Forgiveness is based on one thing—the forgiveness of Christ. The servant owed the king an enormous debt he could never repay. The king did not say he would work out a payment plan or reduce the debt. No, he chose to forgive the debt entirely. The king erased the servant's debt as though it had never existed. That is the basis by which I forgive others because that is the basis upon which Jesus has forgiven me. The Bible teaches that when God looks at His children, He sees us through the righteousness of Christ. The implication is that in God's eyes, it is as though we never sinned.

I love the song that says, "I'm just a sinner saved by grace," but that is not how God sees me. God sees me as a child adopted into His family, grafted into the Vine. Because Christ's righteousness has been accounted to me, then in God's eyes, I am not a sinner.

People will remind you of your sins, and so does the devil. But God will never remind you of your sins. It was His choice to cast your confessed sins into a sea of forgetfulness (Mic. 7:18-19).

Understanding this, we can then go before God not bearing the weight of past sins. Through the righteousness of Christ, we come before our Father cleansed. It is with this pure heart that God sees, and this is the pattern by which we must strive to see others. We are not to see others as people who have wronged us and we forgave them, but we are to see them as though they never committed a wrong against us.

You have to wipe the slate clean. You cannot pick and choose who or what you will forgive. "I will forgive

Jesus Said...

you for this, but not for that," is not how forgiveness works. God never picks and chooses what He would and would not forgive; neither does He offer to forgive some while leaving others out on their own. In the parable of the king, the entire amount was forgiven, so we must all be willing to forgive completely.

I enjoy reading the story of Corrie ten Boom. I have read her book *The Hiding Place* several times. In summary, this book is about a Dutch Christian family who was taken captive by the Nazi regime, which was occupying Holland. Corrie's father was in his eighties, her sister in her sixties, and Corrie herself was in her fifties. They were all carted off to concentration camps. Corrie talks about sleeping on straw beds infested with fleas that would bite them throughout the night. She talks about being transported to Germany in the deep of winter with no heat. She writes about sleeping in rooms with no windows, and about being dragged out of bed early in the morning and forced to do grueling manual labor for the greater part of the day.

Innocent people in their senior years were forced to perform hard labor. They were beaten and abused in ways we can hardly imagine. Her story shows me that the vast majority of us have never been truly offended. Corrie ten Boom would confess that her initial reaction was always resentment, bitterness, and looking for ways to strike back. It was her sister who kept reminding her, "Keep your eyes on Jesus."

After a time, Corrie and her sister were transported to another concentration camp. The conditions in the first camp were terrible, but the second camp proved to be much worse. Corrie continued to be angry, and her sister would remind her that the Bible says, "In everything give thanks" (1 Thess. 5:16).

Corrie's response was, "You expect me to give thanks for fleas?" Then a few months later, she realized the German guards refused to come into their rooms to harass and abuse them. Why? Because of the fleas! Corrie suddenly realized she could give thanks in everything.

Corrie's father and sister eventually died in prison. However, Corrie was released through a clerical error—an error she believed was purely the hand of God. One week after her release, everyone in Corrie's classification was executed in the gas chamber. God spared her for the destiny He had for her life.

Years later, Corrie returned to Germany to testify in a church about how God kept her through this horrible ordeal. As Corrie entered the church, she recounts seeing "him" sitting there. The "him" was one of the guards from the concentration camp. She remembered how mean and cruel this man had been. She could tell by looking at this man's eyes precisely who he was.

Now, Corrie is standing before the crowd and preaching; all the while on the inside, she is wrestling with the anger welling up in her heart. She shares how her sister and father died at the hands of men like him. She remembers the beatings and the abuse she endured. As she speaks, Corrie sees this man (who was at the center of this abuse) listening to her every word.

Jesus Said...

Corrie concludes her message wondering what the man will do after the service is completed. She grows nervous as people line up to meet her because she sees the man step into the line. She can feel the tension rise inside of her as each person passes and *he* draws closer. Finally, it is the man's turn to greet Corrie. He stands before her and says, "Frauline, I am so glad to know Jesus has forgiven me of my sins. Will you forgive me?"

Corrie's flesh was saying no, but in her spirit she prayed, "Lord, help me." Before she realized what was happening, her hand embraced his hands as tears rolled down their faces. The grace of God was extended to both of them.

Here is the point: You cannot forgive people in your strength; it has to be by the grace of God. It is not our forgiveness because that is shallow and will not last, but it is the grace of God that flows to you and through you. His grace will provide forgiveness to those who have wronged you.

SERMON STARTER
Jesus said: "You Have to Forgive"
Matthew 18:23-35

Jesus' parable in Matthew 18 is a result of Simon Peter asking, "How many times a day must I forgive my brother? Seven times?" (see v. 21). The truth is, it is virtually impossible to make it through a single day without someone offending you.

1. **Jesus did not say the offender is innocent.**
   A. Just because you forgive someone does not mean they are not guilty of offenses.
   B. Having been freed by God's forgiveness, we cannot let our unwillingness to forgive put us in prison.
   C. God does not bless the unforgiving heart. Remember the story of Joseph.

2. **Jesus did not say forgiving the offender means you do not have to be wary of him or her in the future.**
   A. Forgiveness is an issue of the heart, but it does not nullify using your head.
   B. We can forgive today, but it does not mean we put ourselves in a position to be taken advantage of tomorrow.
   C. I may forgive you for breaking a promise yesterday, but that does not mean I will cling to a promise you make me tomorrow.

3. **Jesus never said to forgive only when someone asks for it.**
   A. There will be times people cannot or will not be able to ask you for your forgiveness.
   B. Jesus taught in the Sermon on the Mount that we should settle our accounts *quickly.*
   C. You cannot pick and choose who or what you will forgive.

Then He said to His disciples, "Therefore I say to you, do not worry about your life, what you will eat; nor about the body, what you will put on. Life is more than food, and the body is more than clothing. Consider the ravens, for they neither sow nor reap, which have neither storehouse nor barn; and God feeds them. Of how much more value are you than the birds? And which of you by worrying can add one cubit to his stature? If you then are not able to do the least, why are you anxious for the rest? Consider the lilies, how they grow: they neither toil nor spin; and yet I say to you, even Solomon in all his glory was not arrayed like one of these. If then God so clothes the grass, which today is in the field and tomorrow is thrown into the oven, how much more will He clothe you, O you of little faith?

"And do not seek what you should eat or what you should drink, nor have an anxious mind. For all these things the nations of the world

Jesus Said...

seek after, and your Father knows that you need these things. But seek the kingdom of God, and all these things shall be added to you" (Luke 12:22-31).

Have you ever considered what we lost when Adam and Eve fell in the Garden of Eden? Have you taken the time to review the depth of the human condition into which they plunged us? For instance, when the Fall came, they forfeited the right and privilege to be close friends with God. Before the Fall, they would walk with God in the cool of the day and converse with Him. Immediately after the Fall, they lost the privilege to be the friends of God. They lost the right to live in a place of unending joy. They could no longer live in the perfect environment—the Garden of Eden—a place where they would never lack anything.

They also lost the right to have dominion over the earth. Instantly, a curse was pronounced over the planet that made even the weather uncertain. The Bible says all of calamities we experience in nature are a part of that curse pronounced on Earth. Paul said the earth is "groaning"; it is pleading with God for the day of redemption that will free our planet from this curse (Rom. 8:22).

The woman was placed under a curse, as the Lord said in Genesis 3:16: "I will greatly multiply your sorrow and your conception; in pain you shall bring forth children; your desire shall be for your husband, and he shall rule over you." All the moms out there know this is true!

The man was cursed, as God declared in verses 17-19: "Because you have heeded the voice of your wife, and have eaten from the tree of which I commanded you, saying, 'You shall not eat of it': Cursed is the ground for your sake; in toil you shall eat of it all the days of your life. Both thorns and thistles it shall bring forth for you, and you shall eat the herb of the field. In the sweat of your face you shall eat bread till you return to the ground, for out of it you were taken; for dust you are, and to dust you shall return."

Perhaps, debatably, the most significant impact of the Fall was not what God pronounced as curses, but what transpired at the moment of the Fall. The Bible says when they ate of the forbidden fruit, suddenly their eyes were opened, and they immediately understood something was wrong. They understood they were sinful creatures who had sinned against a holy God.

At that moment, there was ushered into their heart, mind, and spirit something they had never experienced before: worry, fear, and anxiety.

Adam and Eve had never been instructed that they needed to cover up their sin. But almost instinctively fear told them they needed to hide their sin, lest it was exposed. The Bible says when God showed up to talk to Adam and Eve, they hid from Him. No doubt, the spirit of worry and fear had taken over their life (see vv. 7-12). Adam was now forced to hide from the very One with whom he used to walk.

Worry, anxiety, and fear have been the natural state of the human condition since Adam and Eve's sin; it is

Jesus Said...

as natural as breathing. We North Americans, some of the wealthiest people on earth, are consumed with fear and worry. Meanwhile, the poorest people in the world are also bound by the same spirit. People are born with a proclivity to worry and live in fear. This is part of our natural, carnal condition. Despite our best efforts or moments of escape, we always come back to who we are—people who worry and live under stress.

The impact of worry, anxiety, and stress are devastating. I recently spoke to someone about two individuals he had been working with who had suffered heart attacks. He asked each of them what were the major factors that contributed to their condition. They both said the same thing: "stuff eating them up on the inside." It is a proven medical fact that worry, anxiety, and stress eat away at our minds and debilitate our bodies.

When these three elements work together, they are so powerful they can bring entire economies to their knees. National economies hinge on "consumer confidence"—what people are worried about happening as much as what is really happening. Markets can drop hundreds of points, and analysts will tell you that it is "market worries," not "market reality."

Jesus Christ entered a world bound by worry, fear, and anxiety. He was sent by God to pay for the sins of the whole world for all time. Jesus came to set captives free, and to offer us redemption for all of our sins. In one moment, His divine blood satisfied the payment for your sins and mine! Jesus came to restore the human

"Do Not Worry About It"

species to its original condition. Some theologians called it *recapitulation*, which means "to place back to the original order the way things were."

The first man, Adam, forfeited our rights as children of God, which included the rights to be God's friend and live with a hope of eternal life. Adam relinquished the rights to live with joy, bliss, and prosperity, knowing that God would be our God, and we would be His people. Adam gave up our right to have authority over the earth. However, when the Second Adam (Jesus Christ) came, He bled and died, and rose from the grave to restore to the fallen race the right to be friends of God.

More than the friends of God, Jesus gave us the right to be the sons and daughters of God! It is not of what we have done, but what Jesus Christ has done, that we can wake up every morning and say God is my friend, not my enemy. It is through Christ that we can know God is for us and not against us. Jesus Christ restored the rights of authority in the kingdom of God. And Jesus also came to deliver us from our carnal conditions of worry, anxiety, and stress.

In Luke 12:22-31, Jesus gave an interesting command. He said, "Do not worry about your life." The command came in the middle of a conversation He was having with His disciples. He had been telling the story of the rich fool. This man looked at his empire and said to himself, "I'm doing pretty good." He did an accounting of his assets, and concluded he had enjoyed a good run over the past several years. So, the man decided to build bigger barns to gather more stuff. He looked over all he had accumulated and declared, "Soul, you have many goods laid up for many years; take your ease; eat, drink, and be merry" (v. 19).

Sadly, the Lord called this man a fool! "But God said to him, 'Fool! This night your soul will be required of you; then whose will those things be which you have provided?'" (v. 20).

How ironic! In our economy, any man who would want to expand his business would be a cause for celebration. He would be called a "driven" man. We would put him on the front page of the financial section of the news and aspire to be like him. However, Jesus called that man a fool. He was not considered a fool because he was growing and expanding; rather, because he believed the age-old lie that gathering more stuff would lead to a life of contentment and satisfaction. He was not the first, and will not be the last to think such foolishness!

John D. Rockefeller was one of the wealthiest people who ever lived. When he was asked how much money is enough money, his reply was chilling: "a little bit more." He was worth more than anyone could count; but he was living proof that when you are obsessively driven for more, then regardless of how much you have, you will never be satisfied.

Concluding the story, Jesus instantly turns to His disciples and announces, "Do not worry about your life!" Perhaps He is pointing to the poisoned mind-set of the rich fool. Maybe He is pointing to the truth that

"Do Not Worry About It"

when you live to accumulate as much as you can, then the more you have, the more you have to worry over. Consider the more you gain is the same "more" that weighs on your mind. Your mind becomes obsessed with the "more." How will you keep it? What if you lose it? What if someone steals it? The list of questions and concerns can keep you awake for hours on end!

Our church has a retirement community attached to our property. Recently I was able to have lunch with my parents and another couple who also live on the property. This other couple had built a beautiful sunroom addition to their townhome, with windows and bookcases and other impressive features. Suddenly, everyone at the table began to tell me I needed to add a sunroom on the back of my house too. (Note: None of them were offering financial support for the proposed project!)

While they were making their arguments, here is what was running through my mind: *That's what I need—another floor to sweep; more windows to clean; more lights to turn off before bedtime; and more areas that need dusting.* I was quick to reply that while I was glad for what they had, no thanks, I did not need a sunroom. While having things can be nice, I remembered, *The more you get, the more there is to worry over.*

After telling the parable and giving the command "Do not worry," Jesus points at the ravens. His point reveals ravens do not build bigger barns. When you find the ravens' nest, you will not find additions to the nest. Ravens' nests do not have storage units in the top of the tree filled with stuff that used to be in the nest. Most ravens do not have two nests (one at the lake, mountains, etc.). This is not to say we should not have these things; but hopefully, the obvious point is: the more you have, the more you have to worry over!

Jesus said to look at the ravens; they do not build barns, but our Father feeds them every day. How much does He feed them? Enough! Your Father makes it His responsibility to make sure that whatever they need, they will have it. Then Jesus said, "Are you not more valuable to Him than the birds?" I am not saying it is a sin to get more; I hope you get everything God has for you. I am saying you must be very careful because there is a trap laid for each of us. The Bible is clear that God has given you all things richly to enjoy (1 Tim. 6:17). There is nothing wrong with having things, as long as things don't have you!

Possessions can steal your attention and your joy. If you want to live without worry, stress, or anxiety, focus your attention on Christ. If you focus on things, you will lose the joy of knowing Christ alone is the supplier of all your needs.

Now, why did Jesus choose ravens? Of all the birds, why ravens? I could connect to this story better if the Lord had said, "Look at the bluebirds, cardinals, or hummingbirds." I would have my hands raised saying, "Yes, Lord! I watch these birds every morning; I even have a birdfeeder." However, Jesus said, "Look at the ravens." Ravens are nasty birds! If I found a raven on my birdfeeder, I would chase it away. I would yell, "That isn't your food! I only want pretty birds on my birdfeeder." The reality is, the bird we consider a nasty nuisance is one the Father loves so much that He feeds it every day.

Jesus said, "If your Father feeds those birds every day, how much more does He love you?" How humbling to know you are so valuable to your Father that He will provide for your every need.

Jesus is saying to quit worrying about everything going on around you. Don't freak out if the market is up or down, or what may be happening in the business sector. You need to wake up every morning knowing you have a Father who loves you more than you could ever know. You have a Father who sings songs of love over you every morning, even before you wake up. Your Father sings songs of mercy, love, and goodwill, and He can give you whatever you need for your day. Any day! Every day!

This is not a license for you to quit your job. I recall a story about a man who testified at his church that he did not have enough money to pay the rent, the power bill, or the car payment. The man asked the church to pray, and the church gathered around and prayed for him. The next week the pastor asked if he had a testimony. The man replied he still had no money for rent, the power bill, or car payment; all he got that week was three job offers. The overall teaching of Scripture implies that when you are doing what you are supposed to do with the resources God has given

Jesus Said...

you (health, mind, relationships, means, etc.), you can trust Him to take care of everything else.

There are a few principles which I believe will help us to avoid the worry that so easily consumes us.

1. Do not live the accumulating life.

Worry has dominion over many people because they cannot be satisfied with what they have. This truth is hard, but the truth remains. We may feel it is not the American way, but it is the Bible way. What grabs my attention in this passage is that the accumulating life can bring people to the point they "drown" in their accumulations. That is, the burden of the accumulations drowns the person in worry and stress. You must be careful because, while you seek to possess things, it is so easy for things to own you.

I recently attended a conference where the speaker echoed this thought. He shared a statistic that was shocking to me. He said 90 percent of American millionaires live in worry, doubt, and fear. They are afraid they will lose their money. Here is the danger of living the accumulating life: You don't possess it; it possesses you. Life is more than just things.

2. Accept that there are parameters and limitations in life.

Life has seasons, and that will never change. Having pointed to the ravens, Jesus then turns to the flowers and says, "Consider the lilies; there is nothing as beautiful as them in the earth. Solomon, in all of his glory, was not like one of these." What did those lilies do to become so beautiful? They did nothing; God gave them their beauty.

In the spring, many people will spend time fertilizing, watering, and preparing the earth for beautiful flowers to bloom. Lilies are so beautiful when they are in bloom, but they only bloom for about a week. In their brief season, there is nothing quite like these beautiful flowers.

Jesus points out something I have not heard mentioned very often. He says, "Today they are in the field, but tomorrow we cut them down and burn them." Everything (or a vast majority of things) that weigh on your mind are merely temporary.

Our homes, as lovely as they may be, are temporary. I hope you are successful at your job and work hard at it, but remember it is temporary. When you leave your job, the company will move on, and soon you will be forgotten. You can pour your heart and soul into a career, and within a few months after leaving, there will be coworkers standing around trying to remember your name.

A day will come when I will no longer be a pastor, and there will be a short period where I would imagine that some will regard me as the greatest pastor they have ever had. Quickly, that brief period will end, and folks will gradually forget my name!

Early in 2017, I had an attack of Bell's palsy. I was so excited to kick off that year and had my New Year's

Jesus Said...

sermon ready to go. That marked my fifteenth year as pastor, and I felt a second wind as we moved toward that Sunday. I remember driving to visit with a family at a local funeral home and whistling along with the radio. Then, suddenly and unexpectedly, I could not pucker my lips. I looked in the mirror, and the entire left side of my face was frozen. My eye would not blink or close. When I smiled, one side of my mouth moved, the other drooped! I was totally helpless to do anything!

With Sunday approaching, I scheduled another minister to fill in to preach while I left town for a few days of rest. I remember watching online as the young man walked up to the pulpit to preach. If I am honest, there was a part of me that was mad: He is in *my* pulpit! Today is *my* fifteenth anniversary. Suddenly, the Lord sat down beside me and said, "Son, that's *my* pulpit, and one day you will not be there; someone else will fill it." You have no idea the freedom that came at that moment. Truly, many of the things we stress over are temporary elements of life; these things will pass away!

We had a member of our congregation, J. C. Bowick, who during his season of work was cherished and adored at a major company—Southern Bell. Though he was simply a local technician, the company would invite J. C. to come to speak at their large corporate events. His gifts of personality and humor won him the favor of the highest-level executives. He would have his audience in tears of laughter. In one example of his humor, a fellow employee in the company once asked J. C., "Why do so many Southerners have initials for their names?" He quickly replied, "So that all you Yankees can spell our names!" J. C. was legendary! Yet, I remember the day we laid him to rest that not one corporate executive attended his funeral service. The success and accolades were all temporary.

We allow things to eat up at our lives because we have forgotten this is all temporary and will pass away. Do not let your mind and heart be filled with anxiety, fear, and worry about something that is going to pass away. How many people do you know who will rent an apartment and spend their money on remodeling or expanding rooms? No one! Apartments are generally temporary housing, so we do not make great investments in them. So it is with life. Why would we invest so much in a transient world?

3. Jesus declared, "Seek first the kingdom of God."

In every realm and dimension of your life, seek first the kingdom of God, and then in all the other things, God will fill in the blanks. Pursue the Kingdom for your family. Parents, it is so essential for you not to forget that you have those precious children for just a little while. Sow the Kingdom in them now, because the world certainly cannot fill the void that only the kingdom of God can fill.

It is good to appreciate extracurricular activities like dance, sports, and music. Those things are beautiful to enjoy with your children. Those activities help teach a good work ethic, sportsmanship, and discipline they will need later in life. However, I caution you: Do not do those things at the expense of the Kingdom. One day the music will stop, the dance will end, or they will not be able to throw the ball. When that time comes, they will need something much more. Never sacrifice the eternal for the temporary!

The promise we have is that when we seek first the kingdom of God, our Father will add in everything else.

Do you find yourself prone to worry? A song titled "The Same Hands" says the hands that created our world, healed the sick, and were nailed to a cross "are the same hands holding you and me."

It is time to be honest with God. If you find yourself a worrier, tell Him so. As an act of surrendering your worry, throw your hands in the air and give it all to Him. Give God your family, job, and your relationships. Give God those things that keep you up at night and weigh on your mind when you wake up in the morning. Tell Him You are seeking His kingdom of joy, peace, and righteousness. Tell Him today that all you want or need is found in Him, and embrace the peace of knowing He will provide you everything you need.

The missionary Jim Elliott famously said, "He is no fool who gives away what he cannot keep to gain what he cannot lose."

SERMON STARTER

Jesus Said: "Do Not Worry About It"
Luke 12:22-31

Worry, anxiety, and fear have been the natural state of the human condition since the fall of humanity. They are as natural as breathing.

1. **Do not live the accumulating life.**
   - **A.** Worry has dominion over many people because they cannot be satisfied with what they have.
   - **B.** The burden of accumulating things can drown you in worry and stress.
   - **C.** You must be careful because, while you seek to possess things, it is so easy for things to own you (see 1 Tim. 6:17).

2. **Accept that there are parameters and limitations in life.**
   - **A.** Life has seasons, and that will never change.
   - **B.** Everything (or a vast majority of things) that weigh on your mind are merely temporary.
   - **C.** Do not let your mind and heart to be filled with anxiety, fear, and worry about something that is going to pass away.

3. **Jesus declared, "Seek first the kingdom of God."**
   - **A.** Seek the Kingdom, and God will fill in the blanks.
   - **B.** Separate the temporary from the eternal.
   - **C.** Give God your family, job, and relationships.

So it was, when Jesus returned, that the multitude welcomed Him, for they were all waiting for Him. And behold, there came a man named Jairus, and he was a ruler of the synagogue. And he fell down at Jesus' feet and begged Him to come to his house, for he had an only daughter about twelve years of age, and she was dying.

But as He went, the multitudes thronged Him. Now a woman, having a flow of blood for twelve years, who had spent all her livelihood on physicians and could not be healed by any, came from behind and touched the border of His garment. And immediately her flow of blood stopped.

And Jesus said, "Who touched Me?"

When all denied it, Peter and those with him said, "Master, the multitudes throng and press You, and You say, 'Who touched Me?'"

But Jesus said, "Somebody touched Me, for I perceived power going out from Me." Now when the woman saw that she was not hidden, she came trembling; and falling down before Him, she declared to Him in the presence of all the people the reason she had touched Him and how she was healed immediately.

And He said to her, "Daughter, be of good cheer; your faith has made you well. Go in peace."

While He was still speaking, someone came from the ruler of the synagogue's house, saying to him, "Your daughter is dead. Do not trouble the Teacher."

But when Jesus heard it, He answered him, saying, "Do not be afraid; only believe, and she will be made well" (Luke 8:40-50).

Most sports fans know that toward the end of ESPN's *Sports Center*, there is going to be a "Top 10 Plays of the Day" segment, which is a video montage of the most astounding moments of the day in sports. There will be moments that happened in games that make everyone say, "Wow!" At the end of the year, there will be a "Top 10 Plays of the Year," which is the best of the best.

Consider what it would have been like to put together Jesus' "Top 10 Moments of Ministry"—those events that during His three years of ministry would leave everyone spellbound; those times when the disciples stood with their mouths hanging open in awe. For instance, I would include:

• *When Jesus fed the multitude* (John 6:1-14). I would love to go back and see the disciples' faces when

Jesus takes a few loaves and fishes and feeds so many people. With a little portion, Jesus was able to feed thousands and still have a dozen baskets remaining. I can see the disciples in the back of the crowd, handing out food and laughing as if to say, "Can you believe this?"

• *When Jesus told the disciples to get into a boat* (Mark 4:35-41). Here they are sailing on the open sea, and the storm is raging; the waves are coming over the sides of the boat, and sinking looks like a real possibility. Suddenly, Jesus walks up to the edge of the ship, gets on board, and says, "Peace, be still!", and everything stops. To be a witness to that would be astounding.

• *When Jesus walked to the tomb where Lazarus had been buried* (John 11:34-44). Everyone who gathered there knew Lazarus had been in the grave for days. Jesus beckons with His voice, "Lazarus, come forth!" and from the back of the tomb, they see something moving. Surely, some of the disciples had to be backing up a bit, seeing the dead man walking; and I can promise you, I would have been backing up myself.

As astounding as all those moments were, the text today brings me to what I believe to be the most astonishing moment in the earthly healing ministry of Christ. Jesus is returning to Capernaum, which served as His base of operations while He was on the earth. You will note that as He returns, a shift has begun to take place in His ministry. Initially, people were skeptical and unsure of Jesus. Now, having seen the

Jesus Said...

fruit of His power, people are welcoming and even pursuing Him. As Jesus returns to Capernaum, people are excited, and there is a spirit of anticipation as the crowds began to gather. Among the crowd, there is a man named Jairus, a ruler in the synagogue, and a man of good reputation. He has come to Jesus to beg for the healing of his daughter.

The appeal of Jairus gave high credibility to the ministry of Christ, and to the atmosphere of expectancy that permeated the crowd. People were expecting Him to do great things! We can never discount the connection between the *atmosphere of faith* and the presence of the divine Spirit being able to do *great works* on behalf of those in need.

Do you remember when Jesus went back to Nazareth (His hometown)? There was no atmosphere of faith or spirit of expectancy. Matthew 13:58 says, "And he did not do many miracles there because of their lack of faith" (NIV). The people of Nazareth fit the saying, "Familiarity breeds contempt." The people of Nazareth were so familiar with Jesus that they naturally thought nothing of Him. Why? Jesus was a local boy to them, just a hometown kid who grew up among them. Everyone knew His family, His mother, and His brothers. He just could not be the Messiah!

Can you imagine how the villagers in Nazareth spoke of Him? "Jesus heal the sick? No way! I remember when He used to _____ (fill in the blank)." The problem with the Nazarenes was their knowledge and comfort with Jesus caused them not to be able to see

"WHO TOUCHED ME?"

who and what He was, and what God was doing through His ministry. The Gospel of Luke records when Jesus was in Nazareth, the people took great offense at Him. They asked who Jesus thought He was, coming to the synagogue ready to do great works! Jesus replied, "A prophet is not without honor except in his hometown and in his own household" (see 4:24).

Again, the Scripture does not say He *would not* do many miracles there; it says He *could not* do many miracles there. Even though He was God with all power in His hand, He could not do many miracles there because of their unbelief (Matt. 13:58).

1. The Place of Expectancy

How do we approach God? Do we approach Him with a spirit of expectancy that He can and will do things beyond our imagination? Do we approach Him with a sense of excitement? What do we expect when we go to church? Do we plan to hear good music, enjoy great fellowship, and listen to good preaching? Does anyone come in expecting that when two or three are gathered, He is there in the midst? Jesus said, "Most assuredly, I say to you, he who believes in Me, the works that I do he will do also; and greater works than these he will do, because I go to My Father. And whatever you ask in My name, that I will do, that the Father may be glorified in the Son. If you ask anything in My name, I will do it" (John 14:12-14).

Do you think Jesus meant what He said? He said "greater works" would be done by those who follow

Jesus Said...

after Jesus than those done in His day; therefore, I am expecting that today and every day, Jesus will be in the church, and great things are going to happen.

Let us probe deeper: Have we become so comfortable with what Jesus has done that we don't expect anything of Him anymore? Do we approach Him with expectant hearts? I fear that it is far too easy for us to fall into what we call the "rut of faith." We gather, sing our songs, preach our sermons, and leave about as empty as we were when we arrived.

Recently I was working with a ministry leader who was coming to speak at our church. He is a very successful man both in ministry and business, so he is not easy to contact personally. There is a process and a chain of command to go through before you get to speak to him. Finally, the day came that he returned my call. I kindly gave the standard greeting, followed by the standard question, "How are you doing?" I was not ready for his reply!

"Man, God is so good! You know, I can't wait to get up every day and see what God is going to do. Don't you feel that way?"

My end of the phone was quiet. I sat there dumbfounded. Eventually, I gave the response, "Yeah, oh yeah, hallelujah; me too," a tongue-in-cheek kind of answer. As we wrapped up the conversation, I had to scratch my head and think a minute.

The truth is I don't find myself waking up most days saying, "Good morning, Lord." More often I find myself saying, "Help me, good Lord; it's morning." While that may be humorous, it is probably true for a lot of us if we are honest. Do we genuinely wake up every day expecting God to do something miraculous in our lives? We should *expect* God to perform the miracles He promised in His Word.

Knowing I had to quickly get rid of the conviction I was feeling after this phone call, I reasoned that because my friend on the phone has money and many blessings, then, of course, it is only natural for him to awake daily with that mind-set. I even offered, *Lord, I believe if I were blessed like him, then I would have that same mind-set he has!* It was then the Spirit of the Lord noted that perhaps if I would have that mind-set of expectancy, then He could bless me also! What I am trying to communicate to you is that the *atmosphere of faith* opens the door of the supernatural power of God to take place in our lives.

Let us look again as Jesus is in Capernaum where expectancy is high (Luke 8). Jairus comes and pleads his case that his twelve-year-old daughter is dying. He pleads for Jesus to come to his house. Jesus says He will go, and as He is walking through the crowd (so large that it is hindering His progress), something unbelievable happens. Jesus is walking toward one daughter, but another daughter silently comes up, reaches out, and touches just the hem of His garment. No one notices this; it is unassuming. Instantly, Jesus stops and says, "Who touched Me?" (v. 45). Among other things, this is a beautiful portrait of the dual

Jesus Said...

nature of Christ; His divinity and His humanity are positioned together.

2. The Portrait of Humanity

The Bible says when Jesus became a man, He emptied Himself of the glory that was rightfully His. He made Himself of "no reputation" and took on the form of a man. He emptied Himself of all of His glory from eternity past and future and took on the form of a servant (Phil. 2:5-11).

While He emptied Himself of the glory of God, He did not empty Himself of His divinity. He remained 100 percent God and became 100 percent man, and these dual natures are manifested throughout the four Gospels. In the divine nature, He calms the storm, walks on water, demons are subject to Him, winds and waves obey Him. In His human nature, He gets thirsty, hungry, frustrated, and on one occasion is found taking a nap! Generally, in the Gospels, we see recorded the manifestations of one nature or the other, but here we see both natures presented front and center.

On the human side, there is a crowd pressing and pushing against Him, with one person pulling Him in one direction and another pulling in a different direction. In the midst of all of this chaos, someone touches Him, and in His humanity, Jesus is not even sure who it was. This picture of Christ being approachable and being touchable is beautiful! Hebrews 4:15 declares we have a High Priest who can be touched by the feelings of our infirmities. He knows what it is like to

"WHO TOUCHED ME?"

be pulled in a thousand different directions. He knows what it is to have the insatiable demands of people tearing you apart. He knows what it is to be headed in one direction and suddenly a new crisis pulls you in another! During all those battles, *know* that you have a High Priest who understands what it feels like, and the feeling of your infirmities can touch Him.

Not only does our High Priest know how to be human; He knows what it is to be divine. He can be touched, and yet He is still able to touch. The thing that captures me about this text is that Jesus did not touch the woman; she touched Him. Jesus did not see the woman, yet *she saw Him.* Jesus was not pressing toward the woman; the woman was *pushing toward Him.* I am afraid many of us have come to a place that our faith is at the level of only mental ascent. We place ourselves in a position where we know in our mind that He can heal, deliver, or provide. However, there are going to be circumstances in your life where you are going to need a desperate faith that goes beyond the mental ascent of knowing He can and pushes to the place of believing He will!

It may not be an everyday occurrence, but I guarantee there will come a time when you will need that kind of desperate faith. When life gets desperate enough, it will move you from your feelings of, "Here I am, come and touch me," to a different dimension where you say, "Lord, I don't know if You're coming toward me or not, but I'm coming toward You." There may be times you don't know if the Lord is pressing

Jesus Said...

toward you or even if His eye is on you. But you move beyond wondering if He is coming toward you, and commit in faith that you are going after Him. You will reach out to touch the Lord no matter if He is reaching for you or not.

At some point in your life, you have got to get to a place of faith where you don't need an evangelist, a preacher, or others gathered around you in prayer. All you need is to stretch to the point that you can touch the Master, and whatever it takes to get ahold of Him, that is what you are willing to do!

Warning: A desperate faith is not a pretty faith, nor is it something that everyone understands or appreciates. A desperate faith is a pushy faith and not afraid to step on someone else's toes in their quest to chase after Jesus. Desperate faith is not dissuaded by what others think or say. Desperate faith does not come to touch anyone else, nor does it care who it has to go through to get to the Master's garment.

This woman in our text knew she had an issue. She was bleeding, and no matter what she tried to do to make it stop, it grew worse. According to the Law, she was not even supposed to be out of the house, let alone reaching out and touching a holy Man. She finds herself with this desperate faith weaving through the crowd to get to Jesus. At that moment in this woman's life, "pretty faith" was not the issue. She had already lost everything and had no hope, except the hope that was in Jesus. She believed, *If I can just touch this Man's garment, I will be made right and well!* And she was right.

"Who Touched Me?"

Perhaps, a factor in the struggles within the modern church is a lack of desperation. Life is pretty good for most of us, and overall we are not desperate for anything. Desperate people do not care what is politically correct or tactful. Desperate people grab a limb and hang on, with no regard for who hears their cries for help! Desperate people will linger around the altars of the church after the service is over, praying until (and beyond), even when the lights are turned off. When you come to the Lord with a desperate prayer with one purpose and one frame of mind, your mind shuts off the protocols and opinions of people as you strive for the garment of the Master.

Our youngest son is a deputy with the Sheriff's Department. My wife and I have police-scanner apps on our phones so we can hear him at work. Everyone told us we should not be listening, that the job was too scary and nerve-racking for us to hear in real-time what was transpiring. However, you put your child out there and see what you do. So, we are riding up the road listening to the scanner, and we hear him dispatched to a serious call. There was a man in a public place beating a woman, and he had a gun.

The call was given an urgent status. We heard as our son signed-out as the first officer on the scene. Moments later, as we are still driving down the road, I heard him call out. He requested assistance at the most critical level: "10-41-A!" (When your kid is out there, you learn the codes.) Then he said these words: "Shots fired."

Jesus Said...

If there was ever a gut-wrenching moment in our lives where our hearts sank below comprehension, that was it! I broke out in a sweat, and my wife broke out in tears. We listened intently as numerous other deputies began to respond that they were en route to the scene. The SWAT team also acknowledged they were on their way. However, among all the voices on the radio, we did not hear our son's voice! Not another word after "Shots fired!" Then came the request from another deputy for an ambulance. Another called out to contact the local emergency room and tell them, "We have a level-one trauma on the way." So many voices, yet still we never heard our son's voice. Fear began to grip us.

As we listened, I recognized one voice on the scene. It was that of the SWAT sergeant, who is a member of our church. I knew I was not supposed to contact him. I knew I was breaking protocol, but I did not care: I was desperate! I grabbed my phone and searched for that man's cell number. Jan asked what I was doing and was shocked when I told her I was calling the sergeant. "You can't do that!" she exclaimed. "He's on the scene!" I didn't care; I was desperate.

There are times in your life when you will get desperate enough that you will not care who is offended or that perhaps you will be yelled at later. Let the repercussions and fallout be what they will! I picked up that phone and dialed his number, praying, "Oh Lord, please let him answer." He did, in a very distracted voice, and said, "Hello." I said, "Sarge, this is Pastor," and he instantly cut me off.

"He's fine, Pastor; he's standing right beside me! He did what he was supposed to do; everything is good!" I said, "Bye!" and hung up. Sarge had told me all I needed to know.

I can picture this woman who had endured this serious medical issue for years, and perhaps she has spent all her money on physicians who thought they could help her, yet no one could. What she did that day was not protocol . . . and never mind that Jesus was on His way somewhere else. Somewhere within her, a faith rose up that was desperate enough to say, *I don't have to stop Him, or even have Him touch me. All I need to do is touch Him and all will be made right.* She pressed through and grabbed the edge of His garment, and her cleansing came. How wonderful to have a High Priest who can be touched!

3. The Power of Divinity

Jesus said, "Who touched Me?" He did not know who touched Him, which is incredible to consider. No one would admit to touching Him. What a contrast! In today's era, we would all be taking selfies with Jesus, showing everyone how close we got to Him. Simon Peter says, "You are kidding, right? Who touched You? Everybody touched You!"

The entire crowd was pressing in on Jesus. However, Jesus said someone touched Him differently. *Someone touched Him not with flesh, but with faith!* Many people in the crowd touched Jesus in the flesh, but only one person touched Jesus in faith!

Jesus Said...

The same is true of people in churches today; many people who say they have experienced the presence of Jesus, but they have not truly touched Him. When the woman touched Jesus in the spirit of faith, He knew instantly that power had left His body. In His humanity, Jesus did not know who it was; yet in His divinity, He knew something powerful had left from His body. The divine nature could not resist the touch of faith. When faith touched divinity, the miraculous took place. Jesus responded, "Daughter . . . your faith has made you well" (Luke 8:48).

Jesus made it simple, but we have made it complicated. There are formulas that groups have proclaimed throughout the history of Christianity. All the patent answers aside, the truth revealed in this story is this: *When faith touches the divine, the miraculous takes place!*

Today, stir yourself and awaken your faith. It is so easy to become complacent and comfortable in our relationship and knowledge of God. We restrict Him from doing what He desires. Let a new faith be birthed in your heart. Let a faith that expects God to do exceedingly, abundantly above all you have asked or think or even imagine begin to come alive in you.

Do not be surprised by what God will do. God's power has not diminished, nor has His arm grown weak or short. God is calling you to live every day in the expectancy that He will do in His children all He said He would do. God will provide in ways He said He would. God asks that you believe He is who He says He is, and He will do what He said He would do. God is challenging your faith to believe; only believe!

Now, there is one more element to consider. While Jesus stops and deals with the woman who touched Him, Jairus' daughter dies. The naysayers come along and tell Jairus, "It is too late; she is gone." Jesus looks at Jairus and says, "Do not be afraid; only believe."

Jesus makes His way to the house, where a crowd was weeping and wailing and causing chaos. He asks why all the crying—she is only asleep. They all laugh and mock in disbelief. The Bible then says Jesus put them out of the house. Jesus says the little girl is only asleep, takes her by the hand, and wakes her up (vv. 54-56). What a moment! What a day! What a Savior!

Sometimes you must put "faith-stealing" people out of your life. If Jesus could not help the people at Nazareth who did not believe, you certainly are not going to be able to help people in your life who refuse to believe in Jesus.

Jesus Said...

SERMON STARTERS
Jesus Said: "Who Touched Me?"
Luke 8:40-50

How astounding were those moments when Jesus did the impossible before His disciples' eyes! As astounding as those moments were, the Scripture text today brings us to perhaps the most astonishing moment in the earthly healing ministry of Christ.

1. **The Place of Expectancy**
   A. How do we approach God?
   B. Did Jesus mean what He said in John 14:12-14?
   C. It is far too easy for us to fall into the "rut of faith."

2. **The Portrait of Humanity**
   A. Jesus emptied Himself of the glory of God; He did not empty Himself of His divinity.
   B. Jesus did not touch the woman, she touched Him.
   C. A desperate faith is not a pretty faith, nor is it something that everyone understands or appreciates.

3. **The Power of Divinity**
   A. Many people touched Jesus in the flesh, but only one person in the crowd touched Jesus in faith!
   B. When faith touches the divine, the miraculous takes place!
   C. God is calling you to live every day in the expectancy that He will do in His children all He said He would do.

7
"Jesus Said... THE PROBLEM IS OUR HEART"

Then the Pharisees and some of the scribes came together to Him, having come from Jerusalem. Now when they saw some of His disciples eat bread with defiled, that is, with unwashed hands, they found fault. For the Pharisees and all the Jews do not eat unless they wash their hands in a particular way, holding the tradition of the elders. When they come from the marketplace, they do not eat unless they wash. And there are many other things which they have received and hold, like the washing of cups, pitchers, copper vessels, and couches.

Then the Pharisees and scribes asked Him, "Why do Your disciples not walk according to the tradition of the elders, but eat bread with unwashed hands?"

He answered and said to them, "Well did Isaiah prophesy of you hypocrites, as it is written: 'This people honors Me with their lips, but their heart is far from Me. And in vain they worship Me, teaching as doctrines the commandments of men.' For laying aside the commandment of God, you hold the tradition of men—the washing of pitchers and cups, and many other such things you do."

Jesus Said...

He said to them, "All too well you reject the commandment of God, that you may keep your tradition. For Moses said, 'Honor your father and your mother'; and, 'He who curses father or mother, let him be put to death.' But you say, 'If a man says to his father or mother, "Whatever profit you might have received from me is Corban"'—(that is, a gift to God), then you no longer let him do anything for his father or his mother, making the word of God of no effect through your tradition which you have handed down. And many such things you do."

When He had called all the multitude to Himself, He said to them, "Hear Me, everyone, and understand: There is nothing that enters a man from outside which can defile him; but the things which come out of him, those are the things that defile a man. If anyone has ears to hear, let him hear!"

When He had entered a house away from the crowd, His disciples asked Him concerning the parable. So He said to them, "Are you thus without understanding also? Do you not perceive that whatever enters a man from outside cannot defile him, because it does not enter his heart but his stomach, and is eliminated, thus purifying all foods?" And He said, "What comes out of a man, that defiles a man. For from within, out of the heart of men, proceed evil thoughts, adulteries, fornications, murders, thefts, covetousness, wickedness, deceit, lewdness, an evil eye, blasphemy, pride, foolishness. All these evil things come from within and defile a man" (Mark 7:1-23).

"The Problem Is Our Heart"

I am going to repeat the following statement several times in this chapter: If we are going to build high, we must first be willing to dig very deep.

This is not a statement of Scripture; it is a statement of fact. Consider how the building industry begins a construction project. The engineers understand one principle: The higher you intend to build, the deeper you must dig. That same truth must be said of all of our lives; if we are going to build very high for the glory of God, we must be willing to dig very deep.

In this text in Mark, Jesus is having an encounter with the Pharisees. I often call these religious people the "church police." The text points out that they came to watch and observe Jesus and His disciples. Watching is what good church police do best. I am not surprised to see that this group of people existed in Jesus' day because I know they were around when I grew up in the church. Sadly, they still exist in the church today. They are a self-appointed, self-righteous group who make it their calling in life to keep everyone else straight.

These "turf-shepherds" have it all figured out. Their motto is, "If everyone would listen to us, then everything would be fine." If you have been in church for any length of time, you have seen them before. They think they can look at others (who are not in their little group of church police) and discover those people's shortcomings, sins, and failures. Amazingly, they never seem to perceive any sin in their own life.

When the Pharisees (church police) questioned Jesus as to why His disciples were going to eat bread

Jesus Said...

without washing their hands, Jesus confronted them head-on. This was not just a matter of washing their hands before they ate. No, they were upset about how they washed their hands. Jesus was accused of teaching His disciples to ignore the traditions the elders had established. This thought had me perplexed because I wondered how washing one's hands can be so pivotal that it actually could hinder your relationship with God. The idea even crossed my mind that maybe I have been washing my hands the wrong way my entire life. So, I began to research the subject, and found two schools of thought that shed light on the issue.

The first says the tradition of the elders said to wash their hands with their fists clinched to be sure to get all the germs off their hands. They should make a fist with one hand and use it to scrub the other open hand. The second says they were to wash their hands way above the wrists. Of course, failure to wash their hands in one of these manners meant some terrible form of judgment.

Sadly, the Pharisees based their relationship with God on these types of things. Traditions had become their overwhelming focus. In the Old Testament, God had given Moses the Ten Commandments on Mount Sinai; but by the time Jesus arrived on the scene, there were about 630 rules to observe! Every generation added their own bias and stipulations as to how people ought to live. Jesus points out they were not just limited to washing hands, but they got caught up in the washing of cups, pitchers, vessels, and even how they were supposed to wash their couch!

"The Problem Is Our Heart"

Reading all of this, I concluded my wife would have made an excellent Pharisee. She is a "germ-a-phobe" on steroids! When we travel, we carry three bags: mine, hers, and the bag with all the cleaning supplies. It does not matter where we stay (and we have stayed in some lovely places), nothing can be taken out of the clothes suitcases until the room has been scrubbed down with Lysol. We don't just clean the room; we also scrub inside the dresser drawers! And if I dare to pick up the TV remote control before she has had a chance to clean it, may my soul find mercy! We even bring a set of our own sheets to place over the furniture we will sit on!

The confrontation with the Pharisees (in our text) is not about cleanliness. The problem is, a group of religionists had become so focused on the external performance of others that they missed the central issue: A personal relationship with God is not based on externals but on the condition of the heart.

Their focus had become that you live the way they say you ought to live and follow the rules that had been laid down by the traditions of the elders. Following their rules defined your relationship with God. Sadly, these Pharisees had fallen more in love with their self-imposed regulations than an honest, open relationship with God!

The Pharisees alone were empowered to enforce their rules and observances; thus, legalism became the religious flavor of the day. Jesus said the poison of their legalism was so deadly that it nullified every other spiritual activity they may have done. He said

Jesus Said...

in essence, "Everything else you do is vanity because your legalistic spirit has nullified your attitude of worship." Remember what I said at the beginning: If we are going to build high, we must first be willing to dig very deep.

For many of us, this text evokes haunting memories. Many of us grew up in a Bible-Belt church. I certainly appreciate that privilege, but I will also tell you that in those churches you can find some crazy folks. Generally, you will find two things most people are passionate about in those churches: college football and church rules! They will fight you over either one!

The standards of Bible-Belt churches were deeply ingrained in every member who attended. Even liberal churches had standards, and people were held to those standards. If you grew up on the other side of the tracks in a holiness-church mind-set, heaven help you, because everything one did was scrutinized. The Holiness Movement rightly pursued holy living for the believer, but often the outward observations (based on their definition of *holiness*) were the only path to holiness! The holiness mentality missed the inner work of the Holy Spirit.

With thinking like that, it should be no surprise that the Holiness Movement had a strong church-police presence. Their accusations wounded many good people. I grew up in a pastor's home, and I know what it was for my dad to get calls from church members reporting how they saw another member's vehicle parked at the movie theater. I remember calls to my dad attacking him because he watched football on TV (and I remember how Dad replied, but I won't use those words here). The heartbreaking truth is that many people were pushed away from the kingdom of God by the misguided stipulations of legalism and its enforcers.

A pastor friend of mine shared this story with me. When he was a small boy, his mother was diagnosed with breast cancer, resulting in a mastectomy. This surgery would have taken place well over sixty years ago, and doctors at that time did not have the precision and tools they have today. Back then, women who had mastectomies were practically butchered. This wife and mother had always kept her hair very long, which was the standard in the church where they were members. As a result of the surgery, she was now unable to comb and brush her long, beautiful hair, so my friend's father put his wife in the car on a Saturday and drove her to the beauty salon. He instructed the beautician to cut his wife's hair short, to a length to which she would be able to manage it. Cutting her hair makes sense to me; it even seems merciful.

The next day at church between the choir song and the preaching, the pastor stepped to the pulpit and proclaimed there was an issue that needed to be dealt with. He announced that this precious lady had cut her hair and thus brought a reproach upon the body of Christ (I'm getting nauseated even typing this). The pastor then said the lady who had just overcome this terrible surgery needed to stand before the church

Jesus Said...

and apologize to the body of Christ. She graciously complied, but her children who were witnessing this horrible legalistic act were deeply, gravely wounded. This type of story makes me wonder how many people have been pushed away by the still present pharisaical spirit that exists throughout the church.

In Matthew 23:1-34, Jesus declares seven "woes" to the church police of His day. These pronouncements are statements of grief. Starting in verse 15, Jesus says, "Woe to you, scribes and Pharisees, hypocrites! For you travel land and sea to win one proselyte, and when he is won, you make him twice as much a son of hell as yourselves." The Pharisees went to great lengths to win a convert, then ruined them by placing them in a cell of legalism and self-righteousness.

The point is clear: Be careful! The easiest and most natural thing for a church person to do is to become a Pharisee. Each of us comes to the religious table with our preferences, prejudices, and background. Each of us has our proclivities, and it is so easy to put these as expectations on how others should live. This attitude is not just a U.S. issue. On a recent trip to South America, our missions pastor was asked a perplexing question about the design of a new church building. It seems another missionary group had previously visited the area and instructed them to build a rectangular building because they thought God could only be present in a rectangular-style church! (I laughed out loud when he told me, but then prayed sincerely under my breath that this group was not from my church denomination.)

"The Problem Is Our Heart"

We all come to the table with that kind of mentality, for we all come with the preferences we think should be observed by others. Human-made rules and traditions are powerless to change what is truly wrong with us, for it is not the external things, it is the heart.

Listen to what the Apostle Paul wrote to one church:

> So let no one judge you in food or in drink, or regarding a festival or a new moon or sabbaths, which are a shadow of things to come, but the substance is of Christ. Let no one cheat you of your reward, taking delight in false humility and worship of angels, intruding into those things which he has not seen, vainly puffed up by his fleshly mind, and not holding fast to the Head, from whom all the body, nourished and knit together by joints and ligaments, grows with the increase that is from God.
>
> Therefore, if you died with Christ from the basic principles of the world, why, as though living in the world, do you subject yourselves to regulations— "Do not touch, do not taste, do not handle," which all concern things which perish with the using— according to the commandments and doctrines of men? These things indeed have an appearance of wisdom in self-imposed religion, false humility, and neglect of the body, but are of no value against the indulgence of the flesh (Col. 2:16-23).

The Holy Bible says these things have the appearance of wisdom, but all they produce is self-righteousness demonstrated in false humility, and are of no value

Jesus Said...

against the indulgence of the flesh. These observances do not have the power to change the human condition.

Jesus told His followers they must understand it is not the external things that can defile them—it is what is inside their heart. The external can manifest what lies within the heart, but that is all it is. Also, you may abolish and control the external things, but it will not change what lies in your heart. If we are going to build high, then we must first be willing to dig very deep.

Understanding that the issue is our heart, I have a few applications to make.

1. We must steer clear of the desire to police other people's lives.

Some of the sins revealed in Scripture are clear for everyone to see. Jesus pointed out a long list of obvious sins in Mark 7:21-23: "For from within, out of the heart of men, proceed evil thoughts, adulteries, fornications, murders, thefts, covetousness, wickedness, deceit, lewdness, an evil eye, blasphemy, pride, foolishness. All these evil things come from within and defile a man."

These things do not need any judgment from us; for people who lead such lives bring judgment upon themselves. What is important to note is that we are not empowered to judge others through the filter of our conscience. You may not agree with that statement, but I will point you to Romans 14:1-4:

> Receive one who is weak in the faith, but not to disputes over doubtful things. For one believes he

114

"The Problem Is Our Heart"

may eat all things, but he who is weak eats only vegetables. Let not him who eats despise him who does not eat, and let not him who does not eat judge him who eats; for God has received him. Who are you to judge another's servant? To his own master he stands or falls. Indeed, he will be made to stand, for God is able to make him stand.

Here is my takeaway from what Paul is saying: Don't violate your conscience, but don't use your conscience to enslave someone else.

One example that comes to mind is from my inclination to wear a suit and tie when I preach. Some Sundays when I did not wear a tie, it was pretty comfortable. Then I remember seeing a picture of myself without a suit and tie preaching in our pulpit, and I immediately thought it just did not look right. No one approached me and made mention of it; it just did not sit right with me. For all of the opportunities that I have preached since then, I do my best to wear a suit and tie. However, other ministers on our staff preach from time to time who don't wear a suit and tie, and I never say a word to them about it. I will not violate my conscience, but I am certainly not going to put my conscience on them. The same should be said of each of us.

2. **While we must strive to break free from the tendency of legalism, we must never break free from the pursuit of holiness.**

I believe this is where the church that I am a part of exists today. We have broken loose, for the most part, from years of legalism. We have broken free of the rules, regulations, and thought patterns that, for so long, enslaved us. However, as I look at us, I must ask, *Are we still pursuing holiness? Are we still seeking a holy lifestyle before the Lord?*

Hebrews 12:14-15 tells us to "pursue peace with all people, and holiness, without which no one will see the Lord: looking carefully lest anyone fall short of the grace of God." We must be seeking holiness as part of our daily mission as followers of Christ. We must also take care that our relationships with others are holy. In our pursuits of business and careers, we must make sure those endeavors are marked by holiness. In our quest for recreation and entertainment, the pursuit of holiness cannot be forfeited, for without holiness, no one will see the Lord!

Because this is an issue of our heart, we must start an inward obsession with our cleanliness. This is not about what we eat, taste, or touch; it is about what is in our heart.

In 2018, a flu epidemic spread across the country, and it was intriguing to watch the lengths people would go through to protect themselves from germs. They would wear masks in public and not care what others thought. Some would wear gloves and almost never take them off. We would go in grocery stores and find the sanitary-wipe dispensary (used for cleaning carts) would often quickly go empty. Shoppers were using them up as fast as workers could replace them. Moms would carry huge containers of sanitizer in their purses because no one wanted to take a chance on contacting this nasty virus.

What would happen if we were that obsessed with our inward cleanliness? I suspect no one would have to give us any rules or regulations because if we were that obsessed with inner cleansing, then we would avoid anything that might contaminate us. Jesus said the things that defile us do not start on the outside; they start within the confines of our heart. It is incumbent for each of us to know what our issues are and address them.

3. The issues within your heart will not duplicate those of anyone else.

James 1:14 says, "Each one is tempted when he is drawn away by his own desires." We all have things in our heart that we war against; it is our responsibility to fight those things and not what we think is wrong with everyone else. Sadly, we can become so used to our own defilement that we get to a place we don't even notice it. We were born in sin, and sinners surround us. We are living in a constant atmosphere of weakness, infirmities, and imperfection. This can form in us a most inadequate concept of the hideousness of evil. Outside the Bible, we have no line to measure by, and no way to gauge it.

Several years ago, a fellow pastor and I went on a mission trip. While we were there, the hosts took us to an animal reserve where we saw hippopotamuses in their natural environment. We arrived early that morning, and we positioned ourselves on top of a hill

Jesus Said...

overlooking the river. Dozens of these creatures were playing in the river and having what looked to be a great time. We watched as some of those huge animals would spar with each other; it was a unique scene.

The only thing they did not prepare us for was the odor of these animals. Words cannot accurately describe how these animals smelled, even from a distance. Everything those hippopotamuses do is done right there in the river. The smell was so offensive that we stood on top of that hill with our hands covering our noses. However, the smell never bothered the hippopotamuses. That is their environment; that is where they live every day.

It is so easy for us as believers to live in a naturally sinful world and exist with naturally wicked hearts. It would seem we are so used to sin that it doesn't bother us anymore. We forget just how offensive sin is to the holiness of God. How ugly are those hidden sins that we leave in our heart? Our sin is so horrible to God that all you have to do is look at the cross of Jesus to see just how wicked it is. Consider the horror Christ endured and know that is how offensive those little sinful traits are to God.

We do not need the church police, but we do need to police ourselves. We do not need others holding us to their conscience, but we need to be holding ourselves to our conscience.

SERMON STARTER

Jesus Said: "The Problem Is Our Heart"
Mark 7:1-23

If we are going to build high, we must first be willing to dig very deep. This is not a statement of Scripture, but a statement of fact. Jesus told His followers it is not the external things that defile them, but what is inside their heart.

1. **We must steer clear of the desire to police the lives of others.**
   A. There are obvious sins which are clearly revealed in Scripture (Mark 7:21-23).
   B. We are not empowered to judge others through the filter of our conscience.
   C. We must neither violate our conscience nor use our conscience to enslave someone else (Rom. 14:1-4).

2. **While we must strive to break free from the tendency of legalism, we must never break free from the pursuit of holiness.**
   A. Yes, we have broken free from legalistic rules and thought patterns that enslaved us.
   B. But, are we still seeking to lead a holy lifestyle before the Lord?
   C. This is not about what we eat, taste, or touch; it is about what is in our heart.

3. **The issues within our heart will not duplicate those of anyone else.**
   A. We all have things in our heart that we war against.
   B. We are living in a constant atmosphere of weakness, infirmities, and imperfection.
   C. We do not need the church police; we need to be our own police.

As he rode along, the crowds spread out their garments on the road ahead of him. When he reached the place where the road started down the Mount of Olives, all of his followers began to shout and sing as they walked along, praising God for all the wonderful miracles they had seen. "Blessings on the King who comes in the name of the Lord! Peace in heaven, and glory in highest heaven!"

But some of the Pharisees among the crowd said, "Teacher, rebuke your followers for saying things like that!" He replied, "If they kept quiet, the stones along the road would burst into cheers!" (Luke 19:36-40 NLT).

Consider the story of one object that may be the most common tangible element within all of creation. This item is so familiar, you probably saw one today. You may even have touched one, walked on scores, and depending on where you were, you might have sat on or climbed one. Have you figured it out yet? I'm referring to rocks.

Jesus Said...

Rocks are those solid crystals of differing minerals fused into a solid lump. Some are so small, you can hold them in your hands. Others are so large, people strive to scale them. Children play with them, and adults use explosives to break them up; they are everywhere. They sit atop the surface of the planet; layers of them lie beneath the soil, giving support and topography across the world.

As if the earth itself didn't have enough rocks, in the 1960s we traveled to the surface of the moon to bring back rocks! We skip them across lakes, decorate our yards with them, and marvel at their beauty. However, I wonder if we have ever considered "the story of the rocks."

We preach the stories of men and animals. We tell of great Biblical heroes like David, the man after God's own heart; and Moses, the man who spoke directly to the Almighty. Then who can forget Abraham, the friend of God? From the animal kingdom, we tell of Noah's two-of-every-kind floating zoo. We love to tell of Jonah's great fish, Balaam's donkey, and Daniel's den of lions. But who tells the story of the rocks?

1. The Rock of Jacob

Jacob was the grandson of Abraham, the son of Isaac, and the younger twin of Esau. Although Jacob was the younger child, he was divinely proclaimed to be "the child of promise." Yet, like many people who have been given the promises of God, Jacob thought it was his responsibility to make the promises of God come

"If These Rocks Could Talk!"

about in his life! He took matters into his own hand rather than entrusting them to the hands of God!

Jacob could not wait on God to fulfill His promises, so he acted to make them happen. He became a manipulator within his family, deceiving his father and stealing his brother's blessing. Here is a man born under a promise; yet, when reaching early adulthood he has become a thief in his brother's eyes and a rebel in his father's! This brings us to an excellent point: God does not need help from us to bring His promises to pass; all He calls for from us is obedience and patience.

If I have to help God fulfill His promises, then He is not that much of a God! If I think I must help Him, then I do not know Him in His fullness, glory, and power. The key is to learn to wait on the Lord. Every promise He has ever made has been, is being, or will be fulfilled. Wait on the Lord!

Jacob steals from and deceives his own family. He is then forced to leave home and flee to his mother's people. As he travels, Jacob the "supplanter" (the meaning of his name) finds himself alone one night in a wilderness. He stops at a particular place and takes a stone to rest his head on it for the night. It is here, sleeping on this rock, that the Lord moves upon Jacob in a dream.

In his dream, Jacob sees angels ascending and descending from heaven to earth, utilizing a ladder. Interpretations of the dream vary. Perhaps the Lord was pointing out that the Almighty has agents all across the planet bringing about His will and His

Jesus Said…

promises; thus, He does not need the help of Jacob to bring them about. Then the Lord speaks to Jacob. In His dialogue, He reaffirms all the promises given over him before he was even born. The Lord assures Jacob the things He has spoken will come to pass. He also avows His faithfulness regarding promises made to his ancestors. He issues to Jacob new promises of provision, nurturing, and care.

When Jacob awakes, he is renewed and so moved by the presence and promises of God that he does a fantastic thing. He takes the same rock that had been his pillow, stands it erect, pours oil on it, and makes this declaration:

> If God will be with me and will watch over me on this journey I am taking and will give me food to eat and clothes to wear so that I return safely to my father's house, then the Lord will be my God and this stone that I have set up as a pillar will be God's house, and of all that you give me I will give you a tenth (Gen. 28:20-22 NIV).

Jacob is declaring this rock will forever tell the story of his encounter with God. This rock will always testify to him about who God is. This rock will remind him that though he had gone his own way, there is a God who will not turn him loose. This God will not forsake the promises He made to his mother and ancestors. This rock will remind him that when he had given up on himself, God had not given up on him. To Jacob, this rock tells the story of Bethel, the house of God.

Let Jacob's rock speak to you today. Let the rock offer hope to you who have gone your own way. May it give hope to your spouse or children who have gone their own way and, like Jacob, find themselves wandering in a wilderness. Let the story of this rock give you hope that somewhere in the wilderness, God will show up when they least expect it. God will remind them of who they are; God will tell them of His intention to fulfill the promises He has made over their lives. Let the rock offer you the hope that God will give them their own Bethel, a place where they will encounter the living God, and their lives will be changed forever.

Fast-forward hundreds of years, and we find Jacob's descendants are en route from Egypt, where they have been slaves, to the Promised Land.

They had traveled for over forty years. It is worth noting that, as it was with Jacob, the children of Israel's disobedience and stubbornness has caused considerable delay in the promises of God being fulfilled. One generation has died because of their disbelief, and now their children are ready to enter the promises of God. That brings us to the next part of this message.

2. The Rocks of the Jordan

To enter the Land of Promise, the Israelites must cross the Jordan River, and it is at flood stage. Though numerous challenges and obstacles lie ahead in the Promised Land, those problems are for another day. Now before them is the issue of the day—the Jordan

Jesus Said...

River; at flood stage, it can be 1 mile wide and 150 feet deep!

- What do you do when you are entering uncharted territories in life?
- What do you do when you are walking roads you have never walked before?
- What do you do when you are facing enemies you have never seen before?
- What do you do when standing between you and your promise is an obstacle more massive than any you have ever met?

The Bible says God told Joshua, "Let Me go first!"

The instructions were to take the ark of the covenant—that God-inspired piece of furniture which represented the very presence of the Lord—and have the priests carry it first into the Jordan River. God promised to cut off the flow of water from the north . . . release the flow of water to the south . . . and His people would cross on dry land. But God must go first!

It would be wonderful if, before we step into things, we would make sure God is there first! Before we step into relationships, commitments, jobs, investments, and even into ministries, we should make sure God is in the midst. If He is there, He will make a way; but if we go on our own way, we may be swept away!

Joshua did as the Lord commanded. The priests carried the ark into the Jordan. The Bible says as they stepped into the water, below them it continued to flow away as the flow of water above them was stopped! Then, perhaps a million people crossed on dry land!

After the people had crossed and before the priests could come up out of the riverbed, the Lord gave this order: *Gather some rocks!*

- Gather rocks from the bottom of the riverbed.

- Gather rocks that were witness to the miraculous crossing.

- Gather one stone for every tribe.

- Then take the rocks and set them up in a heap so that for generations to come, the rocks would tell this amazing story (see Josh. 3; 4).

These rocks would tell Israel's children and grandchildren that although they may be unsure of tomorrow and they might encounter obstacles that seem larger than life, if they let God go before them, He will make the way, fight the battle, and prove His faithfulness.

I want to testify to a younger generation—a generation which has college looming, careers in question, uncertainties about relationships—and life in general. I also want to speak to others facing uncharted territory. My testimony is this: The rocks of the generation before you tell the story! The rocks testify that as long as you let God go first, no weapon formed against you will be able to prosper. He will make ways where there is no way, and the enemy's plans will be thwarted.

Jesus Said...

3. The Rocks of Jesus' Day

Now, to our main text. It is centuries later, and Jesus is making His way to Jerusalem where He will be crucified for the sins of all of humanity. For three years, He has been ministering in and around Jerusalem, and the rocks had "seen" it all.

The rocks had seen nature itself fall subject to Jesus' power as He walked on the water, calmed storms, and cursed a fruitless fig tree. They had seen Him take a tiny lunch and feed thousands upon thousands with leftovers to spare. The rocks had seen Him speak to disease and death and vanquish their power. The stones had witnessed the lepers being cleansed. They were present when closed eyes and ears opened. They could give a firsthand account as to how closed tombs were forced to release their captives as the dead were given life!

However, on this day, it was not the rocks who were to testify. As Jesus was making His way on a donkey, it was the people—those who had heard His voice, felt His touch, ate His provisions, and were awed by the power. This was their moment to cry out. And testify they did, as they began to shout, "Hosanna! Blessed is He who comes in the name of the Lord!" (Mark 11:9).

Then the church police objected! "Teacher, tell Your disciples to keep quiet. Tell them this praise is not permitted." Yet Jesus replied that if the people kept quiet, the rocks will cry out in testimony of His works (see Luke 19:39-40)!

"If These Rocks Could Talk!"

Here is the point: It is our time to tell the story. It is our place to give God the praise He is due for all He has done. It is our place to lift up our voice and declare to all who will hear, "Blessed is He who comes in the name of the Lord!"

We must tell the story of how we were like Jacob. We were off course, going our own way and doing our own thing, but God kept chasing us. He never gave up until He captured us in our wilderness.

It is our time to tell how obstacles and uncertainties have been before us all along the way of life. In the face of every challenge, we have found our God is faithful.

It is our time to tell the story that this same God has now come near us in and by Jesus Christ. We must tell the story that Jesus is the Rock! He is the Rock who secures us, hides us, and upon whom we can stand forever.

Unless we tell our story, the rocks will have to cry out!

Jesus Said...

SERMON STARTER
Jesus Said: "If These Rocks Could Talk!"
Luke 19:28-40

Have we ever considered the story of the rocks? It is our place to give God the praise He is due for all He has done.

1. **The Rock of Jacob (Genesis 28)**
   A. Jacob could not wait on God to fulfill His promises, so he tried to make them happen.
   B. If we have to help God fulfill His promises, then He is really not that much of a God.
   C. Jacob's rock would remind him that although he had drifted, gone his own way, and had gotten off track, there was a God who would not turn him loose.

2. **The Rocks of the Jordan (Joshua 3—4)**
   A. To enter the Land of Promise, the Israelites must cross the Jordan River, which was at flood stage.
   B. God told Joshua, "Let Me go first!"
   C. For generations to come, these rocks would testify the Lord brought His people across the Jordan River.

3. **The Rocks of Jesus' Day (Jesus Is the Rock)**
   A. These rocks of Jesus' day could testify of His greatness.
   B. Jesus is the Rock. He secures us and hides us, and on Him we can stand forever.
   C. Unless we tell our story, the rocks will have to cry out!

9
"Jesus Said... I AM ALIVE"

I, John, your brother and fellow partaker in the tribulation and kingdom and perseverance which are in Jesus, was on the island called Patmos because of the word of God and the testimony of Jesus. I was in the Spirit on the Lord's day, and I heard behind me a loud voice like the sound of a trumpet, saying, "Write in a book what you see, and send it to the seven churches.... Then I turned to see the voice that was speaking with me. And having turned I saw seven golden lampstands; and in the middle of the lampstands I saw one like a son of man, clothed in a robe reaching to the feet, and girded across His chest with a golden sash. His head and His hair were white like white wool, like snow; and His eyes were like a flame of fire. His feet were like burnished bronze, when it has been made to glow in a furnace, and His voice was like the sound of many waters. In His right hand He held seven stars, and out of His mouth came a sharp two-edged sword; and His face was like the sun shining in its strength. When I saw Him, I fell at His feet like a dead man. And He placed His right hand on

Jesus Said...

me, saying, "Do not be afraid; I am the first and the last, and the living One; and I was dead, and behold, I am alive forevermore, and I have the keys of death and of Hades" (Rev. 1:9-18 NASB).

My intent is not to defend our belief in the Resurrection. This is not a chapter that tries to persuade doubters and skeptics. The truth of Jesus' resurrection from the dead is a historical fact. It is not a myth, legend, or superstition.

The truth of the Resurrection is a fact of history attested to by countless individuals (1 Cor. 15:1-21). Historians accept the fact that this Man (Jesus) did many great works. He was crucified at the hand of the Romans and placed in a tomb. Sadly, it is at the crucial point of the Resurrection where many historians' acceptance of the Jesus story ends.

We declare:

- Jesus' story did not end with His body being placed in a borrowed tomb.

- Three days after being placed in that tomb, His body (verified to be dead by the Roman soldiers) rose from the dead and came out of the tomb.

- Jesus emerged from the tomb without any intervention of humanity in any way, shape, form, or fashion.

- After His resurrection, Jesus spent forty days with His believers, showing Himself to them, revealing Himself to them, and expounding to them the truth of why He came.

As hundreds of witnesses stared in amazement, this resurrected Jesus ascended into the heavenly realm. Suddenly two angels appeared and asked, "Why are you standing here looking like a bunch of dummies?" (Acts 1:11, author's paraphrase). The angels literally said, "This same Jesus who has ascended will come again in the same way."

Today He sits at the right hand of the Father. Our Lord and Savior intercedes on behalf of all His children. If you are a nonbeliever, I will not try to convince you of something you refuse to believe, but I will tell you this indisputable truth: Jesus is alive! Still skeptical?

1. Reality of the Resurrection

A Pharisee named *Saul* was one of Jesus' harshest critics. He firmly disavowed the Resurrection story and intended to destroy it. This might be a good place to point out that, for two thousand years, individuals have made it their goal to destroy the Resurrection message. There have been kings and other political leaders at varying levels of power, along with scientists and other skeptics, who have tried their best to disprove the resurrection of Jesus Christ. Amazingly, so many of those who set out to disprove the Resurrection became convinced of the truth that Jesus rose from the dead.

This was the case for Saul, who (in his religious zeal) determined that he would disprove, discount, and destroy the Resurrection message. He understood that to destroy the message, he must first destroy the

Jesus Said...

messengers! He intended to wipe out this threat to his beloved religion, but there was a problem. One day as he traveled to Damascus to hunt down Christians, Saul encountered the risen Lord—the One he sought to prove was dead!

What do you do when something you don't believe in is standing right in front of you? What do you do when something you don't want to acknowledge is calling your name and declaring, "I know who you are, Saul. Why are you kicking against the goads? Why are you fighting Me?" There on that dusty road, the former nonbeliever named Saul became the believer who would become known as Paul (see Acts 9).

Paul would later write to the church at Corinth: "For what I received I passed on to you as of first importance: that Christ died for our sins according to the Scriptures, that he was buried, that he was raised on the third day according to the Scriptures" (1 Cor. 15:3-4 NIV).

Paul continued the Resurrection narrative in verses 5-11, listing a considerable number of witnesses who verified the resurrection of Christ:

- He was seen by Cephas (Peter) and then by the Twelve (not to mention the women at the tomb).

- James saw Him, and then all the apostles.

- He was seen by Paul himself as one born out of time.

- Over five hundred more believers saw Him.

Some might argue the people Paul mentioned were friendly to the Gospel or were part of a conspiracy. The first-century Christians held to the truth of the Resurrection, even though it cost many of them their lives! Not many normal people are willing to die for a lie. When your life is on the line, and you refuse to deny the truth of the Resurrection, that is strong validation that Jesus Christ has risen from the dead.

2. Reaction to the Resurrection

The question is not, "Did Jesus rise from the dead?" The real question is, "Since Jesus rose from the dead, how will I respond to Him who is alive?" (see Acts 17:32-34).

Chuck Colson wrote a book titled, *How Now Shall We Live?* To Colson's way of thinking (and mine), that is the seminal question for all eternity. *Since Christ has come, died, and resurrected from the dead, how now shall I live?*

The last encounter in the Bible between a human being and the resurrected Lord is found in Revelation 1. Because John, one of the original disciples, refused to stop preaching the resurrection of Christ, he suffered terrible torture. Church history records that Rome arrested John and took him to the coliseum, where they dipped him in a vat of boiling oil. Maybe they thought, *If we cook this man alive in front of the coliseum crowd, we can quiet the message of the resurrection of Christ once and for all.* But they had a problem. They put him in the boiling oil, but the power of God brought

Jesus Said...

him out of the vat of boiling oil unscathed. People witnessing this miraculous event in the coliseum instantly converted to Christ. What an evangelism tool! Any volunteers?

Unable to kill him, they sent him to the isle of Patmos, where they thought he would be abandoned and alone. Though it looked like he was out there all alone, John testified that Christ appeared to Him in His glorious power "on the Lord's Day" (v. 10). When John turned around to see who it was, He saw what appeared to be seven golden lampstands (representing the universal church), and there in the midst of the lampstand was One likened unto a son of man!

If you want to know where Jesus is today, John has the answer. He is in the middle of His people. It does not matter how large or how small the congregation, wherever some gather in His name, He says, "I will be there in the midst of them." It may be thousands gathered in a large cathedral or a small gathering along the seashore. It may be among a handful of disciples worshiping in a secret place, but wherever the name of Jesus Christ is lifted, He will be there.

John saw the glorified Jesus as "one like a son of man" (v. 13 NASB). Though He had been glorified, He was still existent in the image of humankind. He did not come out of the tomb as a spirit but as human. He told the disciples, "Touch Me; feel the wounds and the scars."

John's Gospel says Jesus sat down and ate breakfast with the disciples (see ch. 21). Why is this important?

"I AM ALIVE"

Because even now, He sits by the throne of God as our representative, bearing the likeness of man. When life gets tough, we have Someone in the Father's chamber who carries our image and thus can be touched with the feeling of our infirmities.

In John's description of Jesus (Rev. 1), He has long, flowing robes and a golden sash across His chest depicting kingship. He is no longer a servant; He has been glorified as King of kings and Lord of lords, ruler over all things. John said His hair was white like snow, which is perhaps an indication that He possesses all knowledge and wisdom. His eyes were like fire. His feet were like brass, immovable and steadfast.

Jesus declared to John, "I am the First and the Last, the Beginning and the End" (see vv. 8, 11). His existence did not begin in a manger in Bethlehem. Before the world existed, He was; and when the world concludes, He will be! When every nation has fallen, every kingdom has collapsed, and every worldly system has gone under, there will stand Jesus Christ, the First and the Last, the Beginning and the End. This is the One we serve today.

What was John's reaction when he saw Jesus? John said, "When I saw Him, I fell at His feet as dead" (v. 17). The importance of this reaction is realized when we consider the relationship that existed between Jesus and John. John was thought to be Jesus' best friend, His closest companion among the disciples. The other disciples learned that when you have a question, ask John to ask Jesus!

Jesus Said...

This next part can be a little uncomfortable for some of you macho men, so bear with me. John and Jesus were so tight that John did not have any problem laying his head on Jesus' chest (at the Last Supper). So now here is John, Jesus' best friend, encountering the resurrected Christ who has been glorified by the Father; and John falls at His feet as if dead. Wow! If that is how Jesus' best friend responded to His presence, how should we respond to the resurrected Christ?

We should respond in awe, stricken with humility that the Great I Am would even consider us. Sadly, the Church is no longer awestruck by the Resurrection. Thus, we are no longer in awe of Him. We are no longer humble before Him. Perhaps the glorified Jesus was too much for us, so we have tried to bring Him down to where we can be more comfortable with Him. I am afraid of the modern religious movement that is de-glorifying the Christ whom the Father has glorified.

We have given Jesus a makeover. We exist in a time where our main concern is making people comfortable with Jesus. I am fifty-six years old and have been in church all my life, and I am still a little uncomfortable in His presence. I know I do not have to be afraid, but I also know Jesus is beyond anything I have ever even considered or imagined. When I see the resurrected Lord and understand how His best friend responded by falling on his face like a dead man, how else will I react except in awestruck humility at who He is? Understanding correctly who Jesus is and what He has done gives higher value to the price He has paid for our sins.

"I AM ALIVE"

Jesus told John, "I am He who lives, and was dead, and behold, I am alive forevermore" (v. 18). That statement had to stir so many memories for John, who was there when Jesus was crucified. He is the only disciple mentioned as being present atop the hill. John was at the foot of Jesus' cross, standing beside the mother of Jesus. John saw the body of Jesus, which had been whipped mercilessly until His organs were exposed for everyone to see. John saw Jesus carry the cross, which was estimated to have weighed 300 pounds. That is a 300-pound cross Jesus carried *after* being beaten mercilessly and being kept awake all night at six different trials.

Jesus was also wearing a crown of thorns, and He was forced to carry that 300-pound cross uphill. If He just carried the crossbeam, that alone would have been 100 to 125 pounds. John saw the agony as they nailed His hands to that cross, but he also heard Jesus say, "Father, forgive them, for they know not what they do." John was there when Jesus cried out, "My God, why have You forsaken Me?"

John was there when the basic human necessity was revealed as Jesus said, "I thirst; I need something to drink; my lips are parched and dry" If you have ever been with someone who was nearing the "other side," you know how dry their lips become and how they crave a sponge of water to be swabbed across their mouth to give relief. That was Christ on the cross.

John was standing there when he heard Jesus say the word that split human history into two divisions

Jesus Said...

(BC and AD): "It is finished." Surely, John thought when he heard those words that Christ was talking about His life.

However, "It is finished" was not a declaration that the human life of Christ was over; it was a declaration that the purpose of Christ's coming was finished. The purpose had been accomplished. The blood had been spilled, and the payment for all sin had been satisfied. You need to comprehend that statement: the sin-debt of all people of all time had been paid! On the Cross, justice met mercy. The Cross was the place where we should have been condemned and died. "But God demonstrates His own love toward us, in that while we were still sinners, Christ died for us" (Rom. 5:8).

3. Results of the Resurrection

The sad reality is our world is full of terrible sinners. We turn on the news, and our stomachs turn and our blood boils. Every conceivable sin is a daily occurrence: murder, robbery, molestation, and on and on it goes. It is no wonder why such horrible things make us despondent as to the human condition.

Amazingly, the price Jesus paid on the cross is sufficient for every horrific sin. However, it is not just those heinous sins for which He died; there is also our sins. The "cleaner sins" we do not like to talk about or acknowledge; the white lies; the fits of rage while driving in traffic; outbursts of jealousy; being greedy; giving in to lust, gossiping. We tend to write off such things as, "That's just who I am." The same blood of

Jesus that forgives the most heinous crime is the same blood that is sufficient to forgive every sin that wars against us.

When I see the resurrected Lord and hear Him say, "I was dead," how do I respond? I must respond with grateful adoration! Who am I that Christ would pay such a price for my redemption? *Who am I, Lord, that You would empty Yourself of the glory that was rightfully Yours, take on the form of a servant, and become obedient unto the death of a cross? Who am I? I'm just someone who must bow before You, thank You for Your sacrifice, and thank You for loving me. Thank You, Lord, for providing the means by which I might be forgiven!*

Jesus said He was dead, but then there is the announcement, "I am alive!" He did not just fall asleep, nor was He in a temporary coma; He was dead. But now, He is alive forever.

During His earthly ministry, Jesus brought individuals back to life. He woke up a little girl, declaring, "She is not dead, she is just sleeping." Jesus tapped on the coffin of a teenage boy while his mother was carrying him out to bury him. Jesus said, "Get up, son," and that dead boy got up and avoided the grave that day! Jesus visited the graveyard of a man named Lazarus and told His sisters, "I am the resurrection and the life; though he is dead, yet shall he live again" (see John 11:25). Jesus walked out to the mouth of that grave and said, "Lazarus, get up, boy!" (v. 43, author's paraphrase). Jesus had resurrected people before, but here

Jesus Said...

is the only problem; everyone He revived had to die again.

But not Jesus! He said, "I am alive forevermore!" His resurrection validates that He is who He said He was, and that the price He paid on the cross was sufficient for every one of the sins of humanity. If He had not risen from the dead, then who Jesus was and what He did would not matter. If He had not arose, then He was just a guy selling a bill of goods. However, because He arose triumphant over death, hell, and the grave, it is a divine attestation that Jesus is who He said He was, and He did what He said He would do. It attests that the price paid on the cross is sufficient for the sins of all humankind.

His sacrifice was accepted, and He lives forever. That is the good news; but there is more. Jesus said, "I have the keys of death, hell, and the grave." The keys are representative of authority. They symbolized the power He exercised when He visited *Hades*, also called *Sheol*—the abode of the dead. Jesus has authority over death, hell, and the grave. Because He has all authority, we do not have to live or die in fear.

How should we respond to the resurrected Lord? *In awestruck humility, grateful adoration, and confident expectancy.* All authority is His, and He is going to complete what He began.

I started this chapter with the declaration that I am not trying to convince anyone of anything, and I am not. But there is a connection or correlation for you, even if you do not believe. Every person reading this is alive. You are alive because God has given you life. However, one day you will die. I cannot guarantee that you will live a long life. I do not know what is going on inside your body, and I cannot guarantee an accident is not around the next curve. I do not say that to scare you, but rather to bring you to the reality that today you are alive, and one day you will die.

The question is, When you die, do you have the hope of resurrection? Do you have the confidence of eternal life? You cannot get this hope anywhere else but in Jesus Christ. You cannot make enough money to buy eternal life. You cannot be popular enough to receive eternal life because people do not give it, only God gives it. You are alive now, but you will be dead. Do you have the hope of resurrection?

You have the opportunity to meet the resurrected Lord right where you are. If you feel something weighing on your chest right now and you will honestly say, *I don't know that I have the hope of the resurrection within me*, you can receive that hope by praying this prayer:

> *Lord Jesus, Thank You for dying for me. I believe You died, and I believe Your blood is sufficient for my sins. I confess them before You. Forgive me, I pray, and come to live inside my heart. I receive You as my Lord and my Savior. I want the hope of resurrection. Also, Lord, I want to live in a way that is pleasing to You. Thank You for saving me; I receive that hope by faith in Jesus' name.*

Jesus Said...

SERMON STARTER
Jesus Said: "I Am Alive"
Revelation 1:9-18

The truth of the resurrection of Jesus Christ from the dead is a historical fact. It is not a myth, legend, or superstition.

1. **Reality of the Resurrection**
   A. Consider the story of Saul's (Paul's) conversion on the road to Damascus.
   B. Read the resurrection narrative in 1 Corinthians 15: 5-11. Many witnesses verified the resurrection of Jesus Christ.
   C. The first-century Christians held to the truth of the Resurrection, even though it cost many of them their lives.

2. **Reaction to the Resurrection**
   A. The question is not, "Did Jesus rise from the dead?" The real question is, "Since Jesus rose from the dead, how will I respond to Him who is alive?"
   B. Read Acts 17:32-34. There were three different reactions to the message of the Resurrection.
   C. When John encountered the resurrected Christ, he "fell at His feet as dead" (Rev. 1:17). What should our reaction be?

3. **Results of the Resurrection**
   A. The price Jesus paid on the cross is sufficient for every horrible sin.
   B. If He did not rise from the dead, then He was just a guy selling a bill of goods.
   C. When you die, will you have the hope of resurrection?

10
"Jesus Said... WHAT IF...?"

Now it happened that while the crowd was pressing around Him and listening to the word of God, He was standing by the lake of Gennesaret; and He saw two boats lying at the edge of the lake; but the fishermen had gotten out of them and were washing their nets. And He got into one of the boats, which was Simon's, and asked him to put out a little way from the land. And He sat down and began teaching the people from the boat. When He had finished speaking, He said to Simon, "Put out into the deep water and let down your nets for a catch." Simon answered and said, "Master, we worked hard all night and caught nothing, but I will do as You say and let down the nets." When they had done this, they enclosed a great quantity of fish, and their nets began to break; so they signaled to their partners in the other boat for them to come and help them. And they came and filled both of the boats, so that they began to sink. But when Simon Peter saw that, he fell down at Jesus' feet, saying, "Go away from me Lord, for I am a sinful man!" For amazement had seized him and all his companions because of the catch of fish which they had taken; and so also were James and John, sons of Zebedee, who were partners with Simon. And Jesus said to Simon, "Do not fear, from now on you will be catching men." When they had brought their boats to land, they left everything and followed Him (Luke 5:1-11 NASB).

Nothing is more frustrating than having expended an enormous amount of energy to accomplish a certain task, only to realize you have nothing to show for it. Moms experience times when everyone is finally out of the house, and they say, "Now I'm going to get this house straight." They get all the clutter put up, make up all the beds, and then get into the deep cleaning. They get rid of all those upper layers of crust and dust and get down to the thick layers. They begin to feel like maybe they are making some headway and things are finally looking good. Then suddenly, like a tornado, here comes Dad and the kids! It only takes fifteen minutes to wipe out hours of labor! Nothing is more frustrating than working your fingers to the bone, only to turn around and feel like you got nothing to show for it.

There are people who try to get their financial house in order by attending financial seminars and laboring through the workbooks. They apply the lessons; and slowly but surely, the bills are paid off. Everything is coming together to the point they feel like they are finally going to be above water. Then the world comes crashing in on them. In one day, they get the news that little Sally needs braces . . . the "check engine" light comes on in the car . . . somebody's work hours get cut. For all they have done, in just a few moments, they feel like it is all slipping away.

If you have ever been down that road in some form or fashion, perhaps you understand how the fishermen must have felt in our text. You can sense their frustration, as there is probably nothing more frustrating than going fishing all day and catching nothing (I speak from experience). Some people say the worst day of fishing is better than the best day at work, and they may even put that idea on a plaque for the office; but I beg to differ. I do not like to go fishing and catch nothing. Given the choice of going fishing and catching nothing or going to work, I will take the latter!

So here they are, frustrated and fatigued fishermen who have worked hard and have nothing to show for their efforts. At the end of a long day, they decide to wash their nets and head home. However, these three frustrated fishermen are about to get the fishing lesson of their lives, and they are going to get it from Someone they might consider a rank amateur.

1. The Priority of Ownership

It strikes me funny that as Jesus walks to seashore and gets in their boat, He does not ask Simon Peter, James, or John for permission to sit in it and teach; He just gets in the boat. He then tells them to push away from the shore so He can teach the crowd.

I tried to look at this from a fresh perspective. I thought: *What nerve Jesus had, and how audacious and brash! Where is His courtesy?* Think about it: What would you do if someone just got into your car and said, "Hey, drive me over there; I have some people I

Jesus Said...

want to talk to." Even if you know the person, you are going to give them the "stink eye." If you do not know the person, you will be reaching for your phone to call 911, or reaching for your concealed weapon, or both.

Jesus walks up and gets in their boat without asking permission. How can He do that? Well, He is Jesus. He does not have to ask permission to use anything we own because, in the end, it all belongs to Him. Here is revealed the *priority of ownership.* An owner can do whatever they want because, in the end, it belongs to them. When the owner of a company walks into an office, they do not have to ask where to sit. As the owner, they can sit anywhere they please.

According to 1 Corinthians 10:26, "The earth is the Lord's, and everything in it" (NIV). I repeat: He does not have to ask us for permission to use anything we have; it all belongs to Him. God does not have to ask for permission to use our business, our money, our home, our cars, or even our children. He has a right to use them anytime He desires because He owns it all.

I wanted to make sure I was on the right track, so I began to look through the Gospels and found this is not the only time Jesus takes such action. On the day He would ride into Jerusalem (what we call *Palm Sunday*), He tells His disciples, "Go to the village ahead of you, and as you enter it, you will find a colt tied there, which no one has ever ridden. Untie it and bring it here. If anyone asks you, 'Why are you untying it?' say, 'The Lord needs it'" (Luke 19:30-31 NIV).

"WHAT IF . . . ?"

Later that week in Jerusalem, He tells the disciples it is time to prepare for the Passover meal. They are to go into the city, and they will encounter a certain man walking around with a water pitcher on his shoulder. They are to follow that man and tell the owner of the house that Jesus will be using his upper room tonight. Without asking, Jesus essentially says, "Tell him I am going to use his room." Who does that? *The One who owns it all!*

Here is some excellent advice: Release all you think you own (but you don't) to the lordship of Jesus Christ. Release it all—your job, marriage, children, possessions, and time. The things we think we own are also the things we think we should control. It is here that worry, stress, and anxiety find access to our hearts, and we fret over the things we consider to be ours.

We would live a much more peaceful life if we would drive to work every day with this attitude: *Lord, I am going to my job, but it is Your job, and You can work in and through me any way You want today.* We should also declare the same thing about our family: *It is Your family, Lord; do with us as You please.* We blame many things on the devil that are not his doing. We never consider that our struggles could be the result of not releasing everything to God.

When you release to God whatever you are clutching, He will always give it back to you. And when He does, it is always with a greater blessing on it than you have ever known.

Jesus Said...

Think about the owner of the colt. Can you imagine being the guy who, for the rest of your life, could say, "You see that animal right there? Jesus rode it into Jerusalem." Think of the homeowner saying, "Do you see this room right here? This is where Jesus ate His last Passover. *Our possessions become sacred when we put them in the Lord's hands.*

Here on the shore are three men who fished all night and could not catch a thing, but they release their boats to the Lord. Before the story is over, they have more fish than their nets can hold! How much fuller would our lives be if we released all that we are and all that we have to the lordship of Jesus Christ?

2. The Power of Exposure

Jesus climbs into the boat, Simon Peter pushes the boat out, and Jesus begins to teach the multitude. You notice while Jesus is teaching, the three fishermen continue cleaning their nets. They were not on the seashore because they wanted to hear someone teach. They were tired, frustrated, and probably stunk too. They had nothing to show for their day of fishing, and they just wanted to go home. Yet, as Jesus is speaking to the crowd, His words seem to find their way into Simon Peter's heart. Although I do not know what Jesus preached about that day, here is what I do know: When He finished the message, He looked at Simon Peter and said, "Put out into the deep water and let down your nets for a catch" (Luke 5:4 NASB).

Peter answered, "Master, we worked hard all night and caught nothing, but I will do as You say and let down the nets" (v. 5 NASB). Simon Peter implies he did not think there were any fish there to find. Yet, he says something amazing: "But because *You* say so." Not because there are fish out there, not because they wanted to go back out and try again, but because *Jesus* said so, they would cast their nets. Wow!

I bring that to your attention for one reason—to understand the *power of exposure to the Word of God.* The Word is so powerful that even when people seem to be ignoring it and not listening, God's Word has the power to penetrate their distracted minds and hearts and accomplish the work of God.

I recall sitting in the hospital recently as one of our staff pastors was undergoing surgery. His youngest son, five or six years old at the time, was sitting in a corner playing his video game and busily "destroying" all the bad guys. The adults got into a deep conversation. We were talking about recent events somewhere, and suddenly out of nowhere the child we thought wasn't listening chimed in, "That's not what happened!" I discovered something that day: Children are listening. The point is, we need to remember to rehearse the Word of God in their ears continually.

The Word has the power to accomplish its purpose. The Word of God is like seeds that, when proclaimed in love, will lodge deep in the hearts of those who do not even appear to be listening! Kids or teens might tell you, "I don't like the church"; "I don't like kids

Jesus Said...

church"; "I don't like the youth group"; "I don't like my teacher"; or, the absolute worst, "The preacher is boring!" They will give you every reason in the world why they do not want to be in church, but do not give up. Instead, *keep exposing them to the truth of the Word of the Lord.* Those seeds will lodge deep into their hearts, and there will come a time and a place that God will bring forth fruit.

I cannot remember a service that rocked my world while I was growing up in church. I come from a Pentecostal church, and we lived for the "rock the world" service every Sunday. I was taught by great Sunday school teachers and heard great preaching all my life. However, I cannot tell you of a single Sunday school lesson or sermon that rocked my world. What I can tell you is *the continual exposure to the Word of the Lord* birthed something I could never escape. I do not remember experiencing one of those rock-the-world moments, but somewhere, by the grace of God, it all clicked. The years of exposure did eventually bring fruit.

3. The Progression of Obedience

Fast-forward for a minute and remember this is Simon Peter, the one who will stand up on the Day of Pentecost and preach to the men and women who crucified Christ. This is James, son of Zebedee, who will be the first head of the church and also the first martyr of the church. This is John, the guy who will be exiled to Patmos, and there he will receive the most significant revelation of prophecy ever given to a man. These are the guys cleaning nets on the seashore that day.

"WHAT IF . . . ?"

Jesus does not walk up to them and say, "Simon, you are going to preach the sermon that is going to rock the world." He does not tell James, "You are going to be the first head of the church." He does not say, "John, I will send you out to an island, but you cannot imagine the vision you are going to get." God never starts with the big things but will first demand obedience in what is deemed small. The first thing He says to them is "Push the boat out," and that little act of obedience opens the door for greater things.

God wants to do great things in our lives, but first He calls us to be faithful in the little things. If we cannot be faithful and obedient in small things, we will never be faithful and obedient in great things. Consider Moses as he finds a bush that is on fire—a shrub that is blazing but not being consumed. Suddenly, he hears the voice of God. The Lord does not immediately tell him, "I want you to go to Pharaoh and deliver My people, and I want you to part the Red Sea." Instead, the Lord simply says, "Take off your shoes."

If Moses had not taken off his shoes, he never would have been heard from again. If you are not obedient in little things, God cannot use you for great things.

One time I had a person tell me it was on their heart to go to the mission field to teach children, and they needed financial support. I commended them on their willingness to go, and then I mentioned we needed more children's teachers in our church. The person immediately replied, "I can't do that; I don't want to miss our Sunday services." So, I did not feel I

Jesus Said...

could assist them in their calling. Why? Because if you cannot be faithful in the little things, who can trust you with big things? (see Luke 16:10).

The disciples push the boat out, and now we see the progression of obedience. Jesus says, "Now cast down your nets for a catch." I can see Simon Peter rolling his eyes. You know there are some things you just do not do. You do not go in the kitchen and tell Grandma how to cook cornbread; you might walk out with a knot on your head. You do not go to a professional golfer and tell him what is wrong with his swing.

Moreover, above all things, don't ever tell a fisherman how to catch fish! Jesus is not giving them fishing lessons; rather, He is testing their level of obedience. Pushing the boat out, that is good. However, will you be obedient when the command does not make sense to you? Trust is proven through an act of obedience! If I trust Him, I will do what He says. Simon says something like this: "Lord, we fished all night, and there isn't a fish out there; but because You say so, we will cast our nets." And, wow, what a catch!

What if we quit trying to explain it, rationalize, or justify it? What if we quit arguing with the Lord and just did what He said? When He says to forgive, we forgive. When He says to trust Him, we trust without questioning. When He says to wait, we wait. What if we just did what Jesus tells us to do?

Simon had no idea how many fish were underneath his boat waiting to be caught. Nor do we know how many fish are swimming under our boats. How many

"What If . . . ?"

blessings has God placed right before us, waiting to be received through our obedience? Peter had so many fish that the boat almost sank. I wonder what small areas of disobedience in our lives could be shutting the door to the greatest blessings that God wants to pour out?

Here is the great ending to the story: It is not about fish. Whatever the blessing you are asking God for, it is not about that blessing. It is not about promotion or prosperity; it is not about money, or even about health. None of those are the real goals God has for us.

After they caught more fish than they ever could imagine, do you know what they did? They left the fish to rot! Why? Because in the end, it is about Jesus. Suddenly they realized fishing does not matter; Jesus is what matters. *These men forsook all to follow Him.*

What is keeping you from the greatest blessing you could ever have? Right now would be a great time to say, *Lord, I give up. I am just going to do what You say to do.* You will never regret that decision.

Jesus Said...

SERMON STARTERS
Jesus Said: "What If . . . ?"
Luke 5:1-11

Three frustrated fishermen are about to get the fishing lesson of their lives, and they are going to get it from Someone they might consider to be a "rank amateur."

1. **The Priority of Ownership**
   A. Jesus does not ask Simon Peter, James, or John for permission to sit in the boat and teach; He just gets in the boat.
   B. He does not have to ask permission to use anything we own because, in the end, it all belongs to Him.
   C. Release all that you think you own (but you don't) to the lordship of Jesus Christ.
2. **The Power of Exposure**
   A. The fishermen did not come for a sermon that day.
   B. Somehow Jesus' words find their way into Simon Peter's heart.
   C. God's Word has the power to penetrate distracted minds and hearts and accomplish the work of God.
3. **The Progression of Obedience**
   A. God will first demand obedience in what is deemed small.
   B. If you are not obedient in little things, God cannot use you for great things.
   C. Jesus said, "Whoever can be trusted with very little can also be trusted with much" (Luke 16:10 NIV).